Advance Praise for
The Mayor of Moultrie Avenue

"*Being vulnerable gives rise to a friendship from opposite sides of the tracks.... We all need friends like Carl and Eldo, committed to learn about life, literacy and legacy together.*"

–Dr. Gary C. Niehaus, Superintendent of Schools,
Grosse Pointe, Michigan

"*Carl's personal narrative is unique, but Eldo's plight is not. This beautiful partnership proves the struggle is worthwhile and that our efforts in adult basic education have an impact. There is no greater pleasure for a tutor coordinator like myself than seeing the alchemy of the right match.*"

–Karen Bowen, Adult Educator

MATTOON

ELDO'S HOUSE

HANNIBAL, MO
183 MILES

21st ST

20th ST

19th ST

CHICAGO, IL
181 MILES

DEWITT AV

MOULTRIE AVE

de BUHR'S
SEEDS & FEEDS

WESTERN AVE

RICHMOND AVE

AMTRAK
STATION

LIBRARY

ST LOUIS, MO
129 MILES

COMMON
GROUNDS

ILLINOIS CENTRAL RAILROAD

LAKE LAND BLVD

13th ST

18th ST

TO LAKE LAND COLLEGE

de BUHR'S
SEEDS & FEEDS

AMTRAK STATION

COMMON GROUNDS

LIB

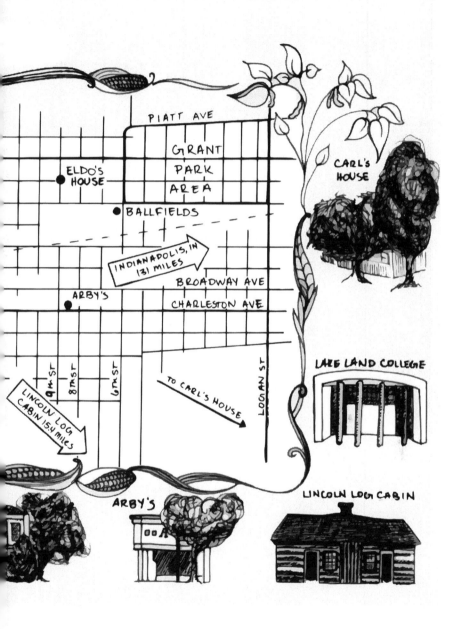

PIATT AVE

GRANT
PARK
AREA

ELDO'S
HOUSE

CARL'S
HOUSE

• BALLFIELDS

INDIANAPOLIS, IN
(3) MILES

BROADWAY AVE

ARBY'S

CHARLESTON AVE

LAKE LAND COLLEGE

9TH ST
8TH ST
6TH ST

TO CARL'S HOUSE

LOGAN ST

LINCOLN LOG
CABIN 15.4 miles

LINCOLN LOG CABIN

ARBY'S

THE MAYOR OF MOULTRIE AVENUE

The Literacy Journey of an Unlikely Pair

Carl Walworth

DEDICATION

In the spirit of lifelong learning

To Kathie, Brody, and Kelli

"*Sometimes we'd have that whole river all to ourselves for the longest time. . . . It's lovely to live on a raft. We had the sky, up there, all speckled with stars, and we used to lay on our backs and look up at them, and discuss about whether they was made, or only just happened. . . .*"

Mark Twain, *The Adventures of Huckleberry Finn*

CONTENTS

Acknowledgments

This book took shape with contributions from many people on multiple levels. The guidance and insight of my sister Candace Walworth moved the idea from a possibility to "let's make it happen." Writer and editor Ellen Orleans joined the team in May 2015. In a weeklong writing retreat on Candace's back deck in Boulder, the three of us worked together to transform a binder full of notes and partially developed chapters into the first iteration of the story. By the end of the week, I not only knew the deer that frequent Goose Creek and Boulder's famed foothills, I also knew *The Mayor of Moultrie Avenue* would become a reality.

Over the next ten months, chapters bounced back and forth from my Illinois base to the team in Boulder. But for Ellen's knack for story development, organizational savvy, and sharp editing skills along with Candace's research and writing expertise, academic connections, and eye for finding holes, the book wouldn't have happened. I love and thank them for bringing this book to life.

My wife, Kathie, supported the process from the start, tolerating weekend writing retreats with good humor and lovingly providing words of support at the right times. By backing my decision to take time off after I left my job as publisher of the *Mattoon Journal Gazette/Charleston Times-Courier*, she allowed me time and space to reflect, to write, and to learn. My children, Brody and Kelli, encouraged the process, too. I'm grateful for a loving family who welcomes such new adventures. Their friendship means the world to me.

While writing the book, I met weekly with Eldo Ealy, sharing coffee and conversation that helped jog and sharpen my – *our* – memory on details of time and place. In late March, I arrived on his front step with a draft of the book, which Eldo and I partially read over the ensuing weeks, sharing the joy of being "characters" in a book together. Eldo's wife, Judy, also graciously read and gave her blessing to the book. I thank Eldo and Judy for their friendship and for welcoming me into their home and world.

Others who read and provided fresh eyes, ears, and insights to the project include my sister Lisa Walworth and Harold Booker of Seattle; Jessica Ratliff of Portland; Lee Worley of Boulder; Pat Hemmett, Ardeth Finley, Sandra Gourley, Bill Hamel, and Tony Sparks of Mattoon; Mary Lou Gaskill of Charleston (Illinois); my son, Brody, of Springfield (Illinois); daughter, Kelli, of Brooklyn; and my wife, Kathie. Tom Vance, also of Charleston, reviewed the Lincoln chapter for historical accuracy. I thank them all for their time, thoughtful input, and encouraging words.

Lisa suggested adding an illustrated map of Mattoon. I am grateful to visual artist Mikaela Fortune of Portland for beautifully transforming this idea into reality and to Lisa and Brad Booker for underwriting the illustration.

Finally, I acknowledge the inspiration of my late parents, Maurice and Eula Walworth, who would have supported and loved this work. I offer deep gratitude for them and for all who supported and encouraged me and *The Mayor of Moultrie Avenue*.

Carl Walworth
Matoon, Illinois
June 2016

Preface

"I trust you. Do what you think is best." The words of my former literacy student Eldo cheered me as I pondered writing our story. We sat in one of our favorite spots, partaking in one of our favorite activities: drinking coffee at Arby's. It was the summer of 2015.

When I signed up for Project PAL's literacy program in 1992, I had imagined I'd stay with the organization for a few years. I envisioned helping a handful of students improve their reading skills, then moving on to another local volunteer project. I could not have predicted the twenty-four-year voyage onto which this decision would launch me, the boundaries I would cross, nor the education I would receive in return: learning about our school system, real-life economics, the complexity of health care, day-to-day survival strategies, and mostly, the many ways of being a true neighbor.

I certainly didn't expect to write a book about my experiences.

Why did I choose a literacy program for my volunteer work? The one-to-one nature of Project PAL intrigued me, as it was different than the group-based volunteering I'd done in the past. I liked the challenge, and frankly, I was curious about how someone could attend school for years and never learn to read.

I wrote *The Mayor of Moultrie Avenue* in part to draw attention to the broad scope of literacy shortcomings in the United States and to make a case for why adult literacy efforts deserve our attention and resources. Even more, I wanted to tell the story of how two people from different backgrounds, people who otherwise would never have crossed paths – even in a small town – joined together for a rich and enduring friendship.

As I drafted the first chapters of this story, I posed many of my concerns to Eldo. *Is it okay for me to use your name? Are there any aspects of our friendship you'd rather not see in print? Any personal details I should avoid?* I knew he and I shared the view that a book about our experiences would be worthwhile – that it might shine a light on literacy and reveal the power of one relationship to make a difference.

Eldo gave me the go-ahead. He trusted me, but did I trust me? While I had begun writing for publication more than fifty years ago – in grade school for the *Newton Press-Mentor,* my hometown newspaper – I'd never written a memoir. Would my years of newspaper reporting – first for *The Daily Illini,* my college newspaper at the University of Illinois, and for the *Mattoon Journal Gazette/ Charleston Times-Courier* after that – help or hinder my efforts?

I knew writing a memoir was different than writing articles and features. I knew it would demand new styles of writing and fresh ways of thinking about my experiences. As I began to pull together the threads of this narrative, what I didn't fully appreciate was how twenty-four years with Eldo gave me a perspective and a grounding that made me better – first as a reporter, later as a newspaper editor and publisher, and most importantly, as a father, husband, and human being.

A point of information: While writing this book, I have paid close attention to the language used to refer to adults who don't read. Talking with professionals and nonprofessionals alike, I have heard a range of terms – including *illiterate, plain dumb, stupid,* and *lazy*. In reality, nonreading adults, I've discovered, usually know quite a lot. Their inability to read requires them to acquire knowledge in other, often innovative ways. Many nonreaders are particularly resilient and live engaged lives. With all that in mind, the term I prefer for adults who don't read is nonjudgmental and direct: *nonreader*.

Of course, not reading handicaps many nonreaders' efforts, but most nonreaders are resourceful and productive. As for the word *literate*, in most dictionaries it is first defined as "able to read and write," but it is also defined as "having knowledge or skill in a specified field," such as *computer-literate*. Early on, I discovered that Eldo was literate in ways that I was not, just as I have strengths he doesn't. I often think of Eldo as *life-literate*.

Finally, in order to protect the privacy of some of the people described in this memoir, I have changed the names of colleagues and certain details of their lives. But Eldo, I, and Mattoon are certainly real. I invite you to join us in our journey.

ONE
Pins and Needles

On a spring day in 1992, I trekked up the worn stone steps of the downtown Carnegie library in Mattoon, Illinois. Normally, I would have appreciated the freshly cut grass and blossom-scented springtime air. Today, however, my attention was elsewhere. I was about to meet a man who, despite attending school through the eighth grade, could not read a menu, road sign, or the forms he was asked to fill out at the doctor's office. My job? To teach him how to read.

"Mister," I said to myself, "you like trying new things, but just what are you getting into here?" My logical mind brushed off my unease. As a newspaper reporter, I regularly encountered all sorts of people in different life situations. What was I nervous about? This was a prearranged meeting in a private room in a public library. I was being introduced to another white male who grew up in a central Illinois community similar to my own. If the meeting didn't go well, I could simply walk away and return to my desk at the *Journal Gazette*.

Yet I could feel my heart ticking a beat faster, triggering my imagination into rapid-fire "what ifs." Despite my six hours of training as a literacy tutor, I wondered what would happen if our personalities clashed and I couldn't connect. What if I lacked the patience and tact to teach another adult? What if this ended in a conflict that hurt one or both of us emotionally? What if I were unable to relate to his world?

Months earlier, I had been looking for a way to give back to my community, and as a writer and lover of words, I noticed a brochure for Project PAL on the library counter. PAL stands for Partners in Adult Literacy, a program that pairs adult tutors with adult students for one-on-one tutoring in reading.

Shaking off my nervousness, I climbed the stairs to a room on the second floor of the library. There, I recognized Debbie Haynes, a representative of the local community college that manages the literacy program. Debbie had helped train me as a volunteer tutor and now was facilitating my initial student meeting. Next to Debbie stood a nearly fifty-year-old man who was about six feet tall, maybe two hundred pounds. A little scruffy, missing all but a couple of his lower teeth, he had a beard and mustache with a tint of gray. He wore blue jeans, a simple shirt, and a baseball cap. He could have just walked out of a factory.

"Carl, this is Eldo," Debbie said.

"Glad to meet you," I said, firmly shaking his big hand. Months later, Eldo acknowledged that he hadn't understood why I would be interested in working with him. His upbringing had reinforced the belief that professionals like myself lived in our own worlds, preoccupied with our own careers, families, and social lives. (As he said this, I pondered what my upbringing had reinforced in me about working-class families.) Further, Eldo had believed that "people like me" weren't to be distracted by "people like him" from the "lunch-pail" world, particularly someone beyond middle age who couldn't even read.

I understood how he could question that I, age thirty-one, a freshly shaven, overweight, bald-on-top professional, could actually care about him. Assessing me in my khaki pants, dress shirt, and dress shoes, Eldo had wondered if I were here just to add something to my resume. Was I serious about helping him improve his life?

Later on, I would also learn that among his friends and family, Eldo went by the name "Butch," a nickname he'd had since childhood. While he and I would grow closer over the years, I usually stuck with "Eldo," though I often heard others call him Butch. He told me some long-time friends didn't know Eldo was his given name.

At that first meeting, the three of us took our seats around one end of the long conference table that filled the room, a table that could have sat four times our group. Settling into old but sturdy wooden chairs, we exchanged more small talk about the day's weather, the coming of spring, and where to find potholes, typical topics for our Midwestern town of eighteen thousand. As we talked further, I could tell from his hesitancy and stiffness that he, like me, was nervous. He answered questions cautiously, being polite but not volunteering additional details. Eldo was not used to casually talking about living his life without reading. I would soon learn that, on Moultrie Avenue where Eldo grew up, family and friends didn't discuss it either.

Eldo was not alone in his situation. Among Eldo's childhood friends, nearly half didn't read or read very little – what the literacy world calls "low readers." This was considered a private, not community, concern. In some cases, even low readers' closest friends and family didn't know about their lack of reading. With this in mind, as we sat at the end of that long, mostly empty table, I imagined Eldo's trepidation at opening up to someone new.

To complicate matters, Eldo's former tutor had recently died. This meant that for Eldo to continue deciphering the mysterious symbol system of letters, their sounds, and their meanings, he would need to trust his secret with yet another adult.

I decided that a straightforward approach was best.

"I understand you were making progress with Ken Watts and that you liked working together," I said.

"We'd been meeting every week," Eldo told me of his student-tutor relationship, his warm smile evoking mine in return. "We read a story, then went over the questions at the end."

"Okay," I said, taking a deep breath and uttering my first instructions as a literacy tutor. "Today is a meet-and-greet, so we're not going to start a lesson. But if you'll walk me through the process for your sessions, I'll try to do it the same way as Ken did. Next week, we can begin with a new lesson."

After setting up our next meeting, together we descended the steps outside the library. The grass was turning a brighter green, a welcome sight after a long Midwestern winter. Tulips, crocuses, and daffodils bloomed as gardeners prepared to plant daylilies, phlox, bleeding hearts, and astilbes to bring color to the prairie later in the year. On that April day, we didn't know if our budding relationship would survive to see them bloom.

TWO
Fathers

My second meeting with Eldo, one week later, was again at the Mattoon Public Library on Charleston Avenue. Opened in 1903, this stone building is a typical Carnegie library, gray stone exterior, tall windows, red tile roof, and a main entrance guarded by two columns topped by a triangular pediment. The classic look and feel appeal to me. Inside, there is an inviting reading area where patrons can settle in with newspapers, magazines, and books. Some patrons visit this area most every day. Still, I can see how the library might feel intimidating. I can imagine low and nonreaders feeling uncomfortable in *any* environment built around the ability to read. Perhaps they are hesitant to ask for help for fear of being mocked or judged.

The committee that started the library movement in Mattoon formed in 1893, beginning work on the Carnegie grant application and acquiring necessary real estate. Deeds on the property show that nine people gave the land for the purpose of hosting a library building. In providing funds to construct libraries like this one, Carnegie embraced a belief that society benefits when people can use freely available resources like books, journals, and reference materials to enhance their worldview. Prior to Carnegie, private libraries were the primary way readers accessed their resources. Like many Carnegie libraries, this one rests in a prominent spot, along the busiest street in town, a block from Broadway Avenue, two blocks from the train depot.

Mattoon's downtown is much like dozens of other east central Illinois communities. To the east of the library is a bank that recently marked its 150th anniversary. To the south, across four lanes of Charleston Avenue, stands a Methodist church whose local history began in 1855. The church has been at the current location since 1902. To the north sits a locally owned retail store. The original Burger King (not the franchise variety) is a block away, with roots going back to 1952. Within a few blocks, insurance agents, real estate and law offices, a title company, a drug store, the post office, and YMCA fill the downtown.

A nearby apartment complex was once the Hotel U.S. Grant, a former hub for this railroad town. Locals once dined here while businessmen plotted deals and visitors passing through stayed the night. Old-timers in Mattoon fondly remember Broadway Avenue, just a block from the library, as a happening place. The YMCA initially was a "railroad" Y, meaning it was used as a boardinghouse by those who made the burgeoning rail business their way of life. The railroads turned Mattoon into a commercial center for this part of Illinois.

Beyond the town's streets, the land was once covered with prairie grass. Now the rich, black dirt is neatly plowed to produce corn and soybeans marketed domestically and around the world. A well-traveled friend once described the Illinois prairie as the flattest place he's ever seen. A family member who visited from Seattle was amazed that when driving along the interstate, he could see the entire train, from engine to what used to be the caboose, on the adjacent tracks.

Mattoon lies about halfway between Indianapolis and St. Louis, 180 miles south of Chicago. For most Chicago residents, anything outside the "Chicagoland" metropolitan area is "southern" Illinois. For those of us living in central Illinois, however, southern Illinois begins when the soil and topography change, about twenty-five miles south of Mattoon.

Climbing the steps to my second meeting with Eldo, my mind turned to the landscape of this incipient and uncertain tutor-learner relationship. Not unlike a music recital, this was the stomach-in-knots moment before the performance or, for athletes, the moment before the game. "Well," I thought, "a little sweat on the palms is good for the soul."

Eldo was on time – an auspicious sign. I had recognized his red Chevrolet pickup truck out front, having seen it last week as we were leaving together. As I headed through the library's side door and up two steps to the main counter, I saw Eldo standing quietly. Again, he was wearing a cap, jeans, T-shirt, and well-worn tennis shoes. No sign floated above his head announcing *I don't read*.

Once we discovered more about one another, this second session was easier than the first. Eldo talked about his family, his wife, Judy, his grown children, Patty, John, Joey, and Tim, and his four grandchildren. I told him about my wife, Kathie, and my own children, Kelli and Brody, ages three and five. We'd established our first connection beyond teacher and student: we were both fathers.

"As a boy," Eldo told me, "I came to this library to talk to girls. I didn't read anything. Nobody asked me why I wasn't reading, but if they had, I just would have picked up a newspaper or magazine and pretended."

Outside the library, he often joined a small group of old men sitting on benches who were passing the time with conversation, some of them whittling with their pocket knives. Those men had been sources of information. Eldo learned by listening, asking them questions, and showing interest in what they were discussing.

"All these years later," he now told me, "I didn't think I'd be coming inside a library to investigate books."

Some of our initial unease remained – neither of us had spent much face-to-face time with someone whose background was so different from our own – but in this second meeting, I could feel it receding. I again asked Eldo about his former tutor, Ken, encouraging him to keep his progress and momentum going. Tutors are coached to encourage. The fragile world around adult students crumbles easily, particularly while constructing the relationship's foundation. "He was easy to work with," Eldo told me. "He was patient and genuine. You could tell he cared."

During this second session, Eldo and I talked about his diabetes and heart problems. Then he told me about an elderly neighbor whom he checked on, making sure she was okay physically and that she had enough food. He told me about his latest visit to the auto salvage yard, where he rummaged for used parts he might need. Next we moved into our lesson.

We needed to set and reset goals, but it was a fine line between getting to the point and taking time to establish a connection. People don't care how much you know until they know how much you care. In the weekly sessions that followed, I stayed attuned to Eldo's interests, looking for information to guide our lessons without coming off as judgmental or threatening. This is especially important for nonreaders who are often sensitive about whom they allow inside their world.

During this first full lesson – based on Eldo's assessment and previous learning experiences – I knew we wouldn't immediately solve Eldo's reading problems or magically transform him into a voracious reader who consumes books of every sort. It was possible, however, for the opposite to happen: for me to do something to poison the process. Making assumptions, sounding dismissive, or being momentarily careless with my words – Eldo could interpret any slip-up as judgmental and send the relationship to a quick exit. So I eased in, emphasizing that we first establish sufficient rapport.

Another huge factor would play into Eldo's reading lessons: his health. Unfortunately, both Eldo and his wife, Judy, had considerable medical problems. Both had diabetes, and Judy, Eldo informed me a few months later, had had a major heart attack. In addition to an enlarged heart and history of stroke, Eldo lived with high blood pressure. With their multiple diagnoses, Eldo and Judy took fifteen prescription medications, including medications to help control his blood sugar and reduce his chances of having another stroke. All this was unfamiliar to me, someone who had never taken an ongoing prescription medicine.

A few times, Eldo confided, he had purchased Judy's medication first, making his their second priority. Sometimes he didn't get his medicine in a timely manner because he didn't have the co-pay. That led to "bad days" when his ability to learn new words and practice reading diminished noticeably.

Low reading, I soon discovered, often leads to low-wage jobs, which are often associated with poor health, unreliable work schedules, decreased food options, and little or no health insurance. Tutoring, like the human condition itself, would turn out to be a more complicated journey than I first imagined.

In our initial lessons, Eldo and I primarily used Frank Laubach's program *Way To Reading*. This series has different levels just as grade-level textbooks do. We began at a basic level. Typically, we started by focusing on a letter and the sound it creates. *This is the letter "b." It has the sound buh, buh, like in butter or best. This is a "c." The sound is cuh, cuh, like in cat or cute.*

We sounded out words together. Then I introduced vocabulary words. We talked about the definition of each word and how it might be used in writing. We found those vocabulary words in the textbook's short stories. We read the story, then worked through questions that tested comprehension.

As the weeks turned into months (and Eldo's T-shirts turned into flannel shirts), Eldo expanded the library of words that he recognized. When he got stuck, he took time to sound out troublesome words. I helped when needed. He often figured out unrecognizable words once they were placed in context.

Eldo told me about going to the grocery store with Judy and how he now recognized words that previously were like a foreign language. We've all toyed with things to see if they work, maybe altering a recipe, trying a home improvement project learned from a TV show, or testing a change in our golf swing. When it works, we may experience a *Yes! That's better!* feeling. I could detect Eldo experiencing that sensation as he saw words come together. The curiosity we carry as small children was revived in a corner of Eldo's life.

While we generally worked through a new lesson at each session, I stressed flexibility. Not surprisingly, Eldo's overall health affected his ability to sound out letters and remember words. His medications sometimes left him unfocused as did his frequent poor nights of sleep. If Eldo felt sluggish or if he was distracted by a difficulty a family member was going through, we spent time that day on what was most important to him. As a tutor, I began to experience myself as a sponge, sensitizing myself to Eldo's thoughts and moods. Nothing compelled either of us to be there, so an accommodating, upbeat approach was essential.

Eldo told me he'd lived nearly fifty years compensating for being a nonreader. The feeling of experiencing words mirrored feeling stronger after an illness. It was the refreshing first sip of cool water on a hot summer day. As for me? I experienced a sense of connection, humanity, and pride in my work as I shared Eldo's joy. Was his happiness contagious?

THREE
Railroad Ties

attoon grew beyond most other small towns that dot the Illinois prairie because major railroad lines used it as a hub. I never saw all the activity, but the older residents say railroad operations played an oversized role in community life. Every place in the community was defined by its relationship to the railroad.

I grew up in Newton, Illinois, fifty miles south of Mattoon, in a house near a single, little-used railroad track. My dad, however, sometimes used the phrase *the wrong side of the tracks* to indicate someone who grew up in a poorer neighborhood. Competing stories offer insights into the etymology of this phrase. One explanation is that in the heyday of steam locomotives, the wind blew the soot to one side of the tracks, which became the less desirable, poorer neighborhoods. Conversely, *the wrong side of the tracks* may simply be next of kin to *the wrong side of town* or *wrong side of the street.*

When I first began working with Eldo, I thought of this phrase. While it is often used as a metaphor, in Mattoon it is literal enough. Mattoon once had two railroad depots. One was constructed by the

Illinois Central Railroad and the other by the Cleveland, Cincinnati, Chicago and St. Louis Railway, or Big Four. A railway history of the Midwest describes 1861–1890 as the period of most rapid growth in rails, increasing from 30,600 miles to 163,000 miles in under thirty years. Communities like Mattoon emerged from that growth.

With the completion of the transcontinental railroad in 1869, small towns like Mattoon were connected with distant places – Chicago to the north, St. Louis, Salt Lake City, and San Francisco to the west, and Indianapolis and Cincinnati to the east.

While connecting Mattoon commercially to distant hubs, railroad tracks also divided towns in both visible and invisible ways. Even in current-day Mattoon, where the railroad depot is now a tourism office with exhibit space, young and old Mattoon residents alike know the difference, socially and economically, between one side of the tracks and another.

As both a reporter and now literacy tutor, I knew that differences often set us apart, be they between countries, religions, or sections of our small town. Differences can prevent us from forging relationships that otherwise would be mutually beneficial. Seeing that Eldo and I were from different sides of the tracks, both physically and socially, I made it my intention to better understand and honor his world.

A solid education is a necessity for most individuals who want to improve their economic conditions and expand their opportunities in the world. In addition, many people view reading, writing, arithmetic, research skills, and critical thinking as a central part of human growth and satisfaction in life. Still others consider a strong education as vital for combating racism, classism, and other political systems that may work against them and their neighbors.

With all this in mind, I wondered, what conditions allowed Eldo to advance into his teen years without being able to read?

By the mid-twentieth century, when Eldo was a student, Mattoon schools had evolved beyond the one-room variety my mother experienced as a child in rural southeastern Illinois. Mattoon was home to several grade schools. In Eldo's neighborhood, Washington School, an imposing two-story brick structure with a basement, occupied Shelby Avenue between 12th and 13th Streets. Washington School served about three hundred children from kindergarten through sixth grade. Many students walked or rode their bicycles to school, enhancing the local feel. Eldo remembers people who took an interest in him, particularly Ralph Ohm, who was on the faculty at Washington before later becoming a local school principal.

With his school solidly part of his neighborhood and with caring teachers and staff around him, how then could Eldo, and many other students, leave elementary school with such low reading skills? The answer is manifold, lying within the school itself, Eldo's neighborhood and family, the economic realities of the time, and the larger society.

To begin with, despite dedicated teachers, in the 1950s schools lacked the special education resource rooms, one-to-one learning specialists, and individualized student plans that are more prevalent today. Consciously or subconsciously, some teachers subscribed to the stereotype that children from lower-income families or poorer neighborhoods were not apt to learn and wouldn't benefit from a teacher's extra time or attention. For these reasons, whether they could read or not, some children were passed along from one grade to the next through what we now call "social promotion." Other times, low-performing students were detained. Eldo encountered both approaches.

When my children were in high school, the administration did not officially track students. Still, courses like chemistry and honors English were designed for college-bound students while the seats in shop and home economics courses were filled by those who would likely receive their final diploma from Mattoon High School or a vocational school. Tracked or not, by the time they reached high school, students like Eldo had already vanished from the school scene.

Compounding the problem, Eldo's family was not worried about his inability to read. As Eldo remembers, about half the students he knew, including many of his own friends, read at low levels, if at all. As a result, Eldo experienced little peer pressure to improve his literacy skills.

In some ways, this attitude was well founded. Mid-century, when Eldo was growing up, most white men were capable of supporting a family and starting a productive work life without being able to read. Men could use their hands to make a living, particularly someone like Eldo who was physically strong and mechanically savvy. He didn't have to read the manuals to make an engine work.

In the 1950s, rural and working class young men like Eldo often started work in their teens. The oldest boy and fourth of ten children, Eldo attended school less and less as he grew older. His report card showed Fs. By age twelve, he was working at Weir's Grocery, one of many neighborhood food markets in the pre-big box store days. Mr. Weir knew Eldo's paycheck went to his family, so sometimes he would provide two paychecks, one for Eldo to have a little for himself. Eldo also helped a local farmer, planting and harvesting crops. Contributing to the family income seemed more important than Washington School, where he was hopelessly behind. When his mother died, Eldo, in eighth grade at age fifteen, decided he was finished with school. As a student, he never saw the inside of a high school.

By contrast, as the son of two public school teachers, one elementary teacher and one high school mathematics teacher, I experienced schooling much differently. In those days, sparsely populated Jasper County had multiple grade schools spread across the countryside. All students then were bused into Newton High School, some riding twenty or more miles each way. For me, the grade school was a block down the street. In my case, I really could have walked to school each day, even through a foot of snow, and not be making up a story.

The more I tutored Eldo and other low readers, the more I contemplated what circumstances create a successful learning environment. In addition to a pupil's specific aptitude and interests, what blend of encouragement and support from teachers, family, and fellow students makes the difference between a low- and higher-performing student? Because my mother taught fifth grade at my elementary school, I likely received extra attention from the other teachers. They called on me often and followed my progress. My questions garnered attention. While I'm sure that Newton had its share of low and nonreaders, I didn't know anyone who couldn't read the basics.

My home situation was considerably different than Eldo's as well. My parents believed that America was the land of opportunity, both financially and academically. Growing up with two older sisters, educational and athletic expectations – spoken and unspoken – filled my house: We would do well in school (we would, of course, learn to read), we would be physically active, and we would graduate from high school and college and perhaps beyond. From an early age, we talked about *where* we would attend college, not *if* we would attend.

My parents strongly modeled the value of reading. I remember them reading books to improve their bridge game, books about Alaska to feed their interest in travel, and countless books strictly for pleasure. Our coffee table held the latest editions of *Time Magazine, U.S. News and World Report, Sports Illustrated, Reader's Digest, National Geographic,* and *Better Homes and Gardens.* My family subscribed to the local newspapers, and on Sunday, we often picked up newspapers from Decatur, Illinois, and Evansville, Indiana, as well as the *Chicago Daily News,* which then employed journalists like award-winning columnist Mike Royko.

Our parents read Childcraft books to us along with other picture books. My sisters remember Dad reading the Trixie Belden series with them. As I worked with Eldo sounding out syllables and learning new words, I wondered what kind of magazines and newspapers, if any, he regularly saw as a child. Eldo said his father read but not like my family where reading was a natural part of life, like breathing. Eldo's father didn't insist his son do well in school, though he taught Eldo important lessons. Eldo remembers his father showing him how to repair small motors. One key was to remember how he took it apart so that he would know how to put it back together.

Beyond reading, my parents encouraged our interest in the wider world by tuning into Walter Cronkite most every evening. I watched a variety of television shows ranging from *The Waltons* and *The Brady Bunch* to *M*A*S*H* and *60 Minutes,* as it came on after Sunday afternoon football. In contrast, as a child, Eldo had no television nor even a radio in his home. Information came from his neighborhood network. Forty years later, I wonder about the advantages and disadvantages of not having a television or radio while growing up. Perhaps the lack of TV and radio strengthened Eldo's connection to his siblings and his family's ties to their neighbors.

Still, as a middle-class man growing up twenty years after Eldo, I can't find any upside to the fact that Eldo's family had no indoor plumbing until the late 1940s. Similarly, I can only view the fact that, as a boy, Eldo took no trips outside of Mattoon – much less a family vacation – as a drawback. In my case, come July, my parents led us on family vacations, a foldout camper in tow. Over the years, we drove to California, visited the American Southwest, and toured American Civil War sites, including Gettysburg, where we camped outside Philadelphia. These vacations showed us worlds beyond Jasper County, opening my mind to the variety of life's opportunities.

My journalism career began in fifth grade, when as an eleven-year-old, I walked up to the publisher of the *Newton Press-Mentor* and asked him if I could report on the junior high basketball games. As my mother remembers it, he nodded, then asked: "How much will you charge?"

With an agreed-upon per-game stipend, I was officially a newspaper reporter. The paper gave me a byline for my reports of a few sentences on each game, complete with a score by quarters and individual scoring summary. Landing this assignment was like making a game-winning basket.

To add icing to the cake, I was sometimes allowed to watch the four-unit Goss press print the newspapers. Watching the gears of the machine turn, smelling the paper and ink, seeing the conveyor belts spill out the papers, I was captivated. I even enjoyed stuffing the advertising inserts by hand.

As a reporter, I was the only one in our family to elude the teaching profession. Perhaps that teaching gene emerged when I signed up to help with the literacy program. Or since I like a good mystery, perhaps it was a curiosity inside me that urged me to take part. Whatever motivation had brought me here, working now with Eldo, I was investing in another person's world.

FOUR
This Is the Letter "B"

I eased into an angled parking space that faced the Mattoon Public Library. At peak times, the spaces were sometimes full, meaning I took an extra minute to drive around the block looking for a spot along the store next door, a half block walk. That is a definition of a bad traffic day in a small town where parking is free.

Project PAL's training manual recommended that tutors and students meet in a public place. Later in our relationship, I would drop by Eldo's house to pick him up, but in these early years, we drove and arrived separately. The library's small conference rooms were well suited for private meetings and personal conversations. After the library was remodeled in 1995, three years after Eldo and I began working together, we checked out a key to the downstairs conference room – a space away from books, computers, foot traffic, and the general library hubbub. The privacy allowed us to read, talk, and go through lessons without the fear of being interrupted by a curious patron. The library staff, familiar with me and with Project PAL, treated us professionally. They respected our privacy while still assisting us when we sought library materials written for basic readers yet appropriate for an adult man.

Again, we were both on time for this, our third session. Punctuality was particularly significant early on, as some students phased out their literacy lessons by simply not showing up. True, Eldo and I were still assessing how this relationship would work, but we liked what we'd seen so far.

I also noticed, and complimented Eldo on, his ball cap. For each of our three lessons, he'd worn a different one, and I soon discovered he owned a collection of promotional caps picked up at auto parts stores and other businesses. I would also learn that he shopped at Walmart, the Salvation Army, or Catholic Charities. *Keep it simple*, I'd find out, was Eldo's motto.

As the two of us squared up in our chairs, I set aside the questions that kept coming into my head during our initial, formal pleasantries. *Will we continue to get along? How will we resolve differences? Will we find the time investment worthwhile?* Instead, as we focused on that day's reading and lesson, as well as the journey, we moved on.

Structured and straightforward to execute, the *Laubach Reading Series* incorporated both our interests. Lesson plans included reminders on the importance of putting students at ease and making sure they experienced success. The sample questions helped identify ways to engage students, and the workbook set out clear objectives for each session.

As a tutor, I had a separate teaching workbook. I was expected to prepare a simple lesson plan, which required reading the article or essay for the day and reviewing its questions. The teacher guide included prompts to help facilitate discussion. The preceding evening, or even over a cup of coffee before the session, I looked at the vocabulary words, read the story, and reviewed the suggestions.

Eldo began at one of the lowest reading levels. Yet the stories geared toward his abilities, while uncomplicated, were written to hold the interest of adults. Typical topics included "accepting who you are," "a look at the solar system," and pieces on prominent people, such as race car drivers.

We agreed to continue with goals he had set with his first tutor. Eldo's objectives were concise and poignant. He wanted to read to his grandchildren. He wanted to read the *Journal Gazette*, particularly the obituaries. He wanted to go to a restaurant or grocery store and decipher words on menus and labels. And in the evening he wanted to plop down on the couch with his wife, Judy, and share a verse from the Bible. He also wanted to work toward a GED, the equivalent of a high school diploma. We reminded ourselves of those goals regularly as we moved along, a way to mark progress.

Eldo's ambitions seemed realistic, an essential quality for goals, particularly at this stage in the process when it was crucial to establish success. As we began that third session, a chill moved over me as I listened to a man twenty-plus years my senior experience the basics of language. On the one hand, I admired Eldo for opening this door in his grandfather years. Yet I also experienced another, big picture sensation: *"How can this be? What in the world, in our priorities, in our human flaws, had led to this?"* It consumed my breath for a moment, but I had to remember what I'd been taught during my training: focus on what we could accomplish and not dwell on how Eldo had missed out.

I imagined Eldo thinking *"I wonder what Carl makes of me of being here."* Normally, though certainly not always, being nonjudgmental is one of my strengths. I'd prepared my mind to remain so in that moment, dismissing my thoughts to concentrate on the work.

While Eldo knew the alphabet and basic sounds associated with vowels and consonants, he still needed help putting those sounds into words. We again started by adding vocabulary words. "This word is 'chip' like you chip your tooth. It starts with a 'ch' which has the sound *chuh*. Let's say the word together. *Chip*." We tried another sound and word. "Sh makes the sound *shuh*. The word is ship."

Once through the new words, we moved on to a story, which he read to me. I helped when he got stuck on a word, phrase, or definition. Next, we discussed the story – what stood out for him, what he thought of its message. We reviewed words that caused him to struggle. Then we tackled a few multiple choice questions that reinforced all we'd just done.

As we worked together over the next several months, I learned to build in flexibility. If Eldo was feeling well, we had time at the end. I offered a writing exercise or flash cards to strengthen word recognition. To add variety, I used a separate reader of short stories geared for new adult readers. A math workbook was also available.

Some days we talked about local or national issues, like our new president, Bill Clinton. As the years went by, Eldo revisited particular local issues multiple times, some of which I covered as a reporter. One of his favorite topics arose most every fall: burning leaves. Some Mattoon residents considered raking leaves to the curb and setting them on fire an efficient way to clean their yards. Others claimed that the practice was bad for the environment, unfairly forcing neighbors with breathing difficulties to stay inside. A few years into our weekly lessons, the City Council put an advisory referendum on the ballot on whether burning leaves should be permitted. Voters in 1998 chose to burn, to allow residents to fill the town with smoke, regardless of the impact on air quality or public health.

Shortly after, the council opted against burning leaves, prompting Eldo to repeatedly remind me: "If they weren't going to allow it because of the EPA or whatever reason, then why did they put it on the ballot? We need more common sense." On that we agreed.

As we moved through more sessions, our conversation became easier. "You probably get tired of my complaints," he'd say often. Or "You may not agree with me, but here's what I think."

"I see where you're coming from," I would reply. Sometimes we agreed, other times not, but both of us saw the issues through new perspectives.

At the end of that third lesson, we gathered our books, Eldo dropping his into a Project PAL bag to carry out to his truck. We reminded each other about next week's meeting, Tuesday at one o'clock. I closed out the session with a short pep talk that I would repeat many times: "I'm here to help, and I'm glad to do that, but your progress is because of your effort. If you stay with it and keep working, I think you'll be pleased and able to reach your goals. It's your decision." Then we walked out together into different worlds, each going back to his own side of the tracks.

On that Tuesday, it was back to the office with a new appreciation for what I had, particularly for experiencing the world as an adult reader. That morning before work, for instance, I had read our local newspaper. Arriving at the office, I'd reviewed a rack of local and regional newspapers before conducting a phone interview in which I wrote in my reporter's notebook. At the police station later that morning, a regular reporting stop for me, traffic reports included people's names, addresses, and in some cases, a citation. A significant arrest generated a longer description. On any given day, numerous news releases flowed through our office. When I prepared to profile an individual or topic, I looked for reading material that helped me ask better questions.

Beyond work, the flood of words continued. At a restaurant or traveling by car or airplane, I gave no thought to deciphering words on a menu, signs on the highway, or city names marking airline gate locations. It all came naturally. To obtain information or instructions, I simply referred to the owner's manuals for my car, computer, or appliances (though the nonmechanical me would be unlikely to do that). I took for granted reading the team names when ball scores scrolled along the bottom of on a television screen. Reading the bulletin at the Immaculate Conception Roman Catholic Church? No problem. Reading the label on a can in the kitchen cabinet? Routine. Locating the right movie theater at the multiplex? Easy.

Words were part of my entire day. At home I read to my son, Brody, and daughter, Kelli: *Sandman in the Lighthouse, Mike Mulligan and His Steam Shovel,* and the *Berenstain Bears* series. I remember reading the Sandman over and over, and before long my children nearly memorized it. They could practically recite it to me. Reading books together was a pleasure for all of us.

While the four of us lived in a modest three-bedroom home on Willow Drive, my wife, Kathie, recalls that a teacher told her Brody was "worldly." Kelli, two years younger, was equally engaged. I imagine that our reading together, along with all the books and newspapers in our house, had something to do with that worldliness and engagement.

In contrast to the barrage of words in my daily life, graphics, design, photos, and drawings dominated Eldo's world. I wondered how he distinguished between the different sizes of auto parts he used when he worked mechanically, the brands of products he preferred, or the grades of gasoline at the pump. How did he manage?

FIVE
Fifty

E ldo started the adult phase of his Mattoon work life on the back of a garbage truck. The year was 1964, and he earned forty dollars for a forty-five-hour work week. He spent ten years on the job, learning Mattoon streets and alleys from every angle in all sorts of weather.

After that, he worked for fifteen years at Clark's Foundry, another physically demanding job, where he made metal castings for industrial uses. The process involved pouring iron into molds. One of Eldo's jobs was turning the molds, sometimes weighing over two hundred pounds. Once they cooled, he took a sledge hammer to knock off as much sand as possible. Many afternoons he walked ten blocks to the factory, worked until supper, then walked home to eat. After supper, he walked back to the factory for the rest of his shift.

One day, he and I toured the former factory site, now a largely vacant building. The roof and exterior walls protect the former factory floor from the elements. It was eerily quiet where once the roar of machines made normal-tone conversation impossible. Eldo remembered every work station, describing who performed which tasks. Often he would tell a story about the person's family background. Retelling the story allowed him to relive the satisfaction of being part of a team that together performed a job well. The foundry workers were family. When Eldo encountered former coworkers on the street, the men called out, "Hey, Butch!" They all greeted each other warmly, catching up on details of their lives.

As much as he appreciated the foundry, the work was hard, and the room was hot. He said in the middle of the winter, when Illinois temperatures often are below freezing, the factory was red hot inside. So when the opportunity arose, he took a position at the Young Radiator plant. "The best job I ever had," he said. He worked there for five years, producing radiators used in big trucks and for commercial cooling and heating purposes.

His first job was baking the radiator cores, a process designed to securely bond metals. His second position involved working with the radiator headers, which sometimes needed to have holes outlined by tapping with a hammer. That position disappeared when union employees went on strike in a 1986 dispute over health insurance. The company wanted to apply most all of the pay raise in the first year of a three-year agreement to the health plan.

Eldo told me that he had believed the company officials when they said they would move the factory if workers rejected the proposed contract. He thought it better to agree to the factory owners' terms and keep their jobs. A majority of his colleagues disagreed, saying the union shouldn't give in to the owners' threats. Once the contract was rejected, the company followed through on its promise and moved the operation to Tennessee.

After Young Radiator moved south, Eldo landed at a trailer manufacturing plant in Charleston, a ten-mile drive. That was his least favorite job. Many of the workers were younger than Eldo, at different stages in life and with different interests. In addition, it was, again, physically taxing work, no longer a realistic fit for him.

Two years into that job, he came home one day and collapsed. He lay on the floor of his Moultrie Avenue residence until his sister found him. Eldo doesn't remember hitting the floor nor does he know how long he was there. He has no recollection of paramedics rushing him five miles to the hospital. He awoke in a hospital room, having suffered and survived a stroke that left his left side, particularly his arm, useless.

After a week of hospitalization, Eldo spent another six months in physical therapy. Initially twice a week and later once a week, he focused on exercises like squeezing a ball to rehabilitate his left arm. He regained enough strength for the arm to be functional. He realizes how fortunate he was to survive and retain his cognitive and physical bodily functions.

Still, at age fifty, when Eldo and I began meeting, his life looked as if it were heading for a rapid and inevitable decline. Along with being a nonreader, along with recovering from his stroke, Eldo wrestled with diabetes and an enlarged heart. His job at the trailer truck manufacturing plant was now over, along with working life. He began collecting long-term disability.

Disability status changed Eldo's life, both psychologically and financially. Having grown up in a world where men typically provided the financial support for their families, it was hard to no longer be the breadwinner. Eldo had been working since grade school: his jobs defined and shaped his life.

Over the years, Eldo has told me he sometimes wishes he hadn't applied for disability status so that he could again apply for jobs. "People don't understand the impact that not holding a job has on a person," he said. "Some people think because I get disability, I've got it made. Well, I don't. I've worked all my life, that's what I know, and it's hard to adjust." Furthermore, the disability payments don't fully cover Eldo and Judy's expenses, especially their medical bills. After he qualified for disability, Eldo began to fix lawn mowers and help neighbors with simple household construction projects, but that only brought in a little extra. Often he did – and still does – much of the work for free.

To better understand Eldo's larger life picture, I learned more about the government's disability program. Long-term disability became part of the Social Security system in 1956. As part of disability payments, the Social Security agency determines if individuals can physically continue to do the type of work they've done in their past. If not, the agency assesses if they can do other jobs based on their work history and education level. Those deemed unfit to work are considered disabled, making them eligible for a monthly stipend and related medical benefits, provided the person continues to be disabled and unable to earn income. The system limits what a participant can earn and remain eligible for the benefits. For Eldo, this meant if he were to take a job, it would jeopardize his disability. Should the job then not work out, he would be out of work and out of a monthly check.

Eldo's stroke was a wake-up call and his response to it – choosing to learn to read – was a testament to his strong will. When he'd begun with Project PAL, he had worked his last official job, and therefore he had no financial incentive to learn to read. Yet the yearning inside pushed him toward more learning.

The cause, effect, and general connections between Eldo's compromised health, his inability to read, and his stressful personal cash flow are complicated, but they certainly affect one another. On the first day I met with Eldo, he told me that, based on his heart condition, he'd been given a harrowing (but what proved to be inaccurate) prognosis of less than a year to live. After receiving this prognosis in his late forties, it would have been easy for Eldo to surrender to an isolated life on Moultrie Avenue. Instead, he opened a new door.

Why it was important to him is more intangible than tangible. Eldo said that at one point in his working life, his inability to read caused him to pass on applying for a position as a union foreman at the Young Radiator plant. Deeper down, beyond money and career opportunities, Eldo recognized a gap in his life. He now had the time to take one more shot at filling this void. Learning to read, he felt, would add to his sense of self-worth. He was right. His tutoring sessions provided a positive experience in his world. Reflecting on Eldo's choice, I now see that becoming a literacy tutor helped me fill a void of my own by widening my life experiences.

Further, a common denominator for Eldo and me was turning fifty. We reached fifty some eighteen years apart, Eldo in 1993 and me in 2011. For each of us, it was more than another candle on the birthday cake. The day my invitation to join the American Association of Retired Persons (AARP) arrived, I took a pair of scissors and cut the membership card to pieces. There are better ways to qualify for hotel discounts than be associated with a group whose mission is lobbying for the issues of retired people. *Stay young at heart*, I told myself. *Retain an adventurous spirit and open mind.* In my life, age fifty was when I became restless with being a manager at my newspaper. I yearned to explore my writing roots and my independent streak and to set off on a different life path, which is still a work in progress.

One thing I knew clearly at age fifty was that I needed to change my physical fitness. I had played competitive athletics in high school, but in the succeeding years I had inconsistent spurts of physical activity. I had allowed myself to carry fifty-plus extra pounds for many years in adulthood, getting little regular exercise and adopting an "anything goes" diet. From past experience, I knew I would feel better and have more energy to explore my interests and participate in life by adding regular exercise to my day and using common sense in my diet.

This time I employed a new tactic: I used a trainer to design and update a workout regimen. That helped me get serious about steady cardio and weight work, along with moderation on desserts, bread, and alcohol. At least four times a week, I lifted weights or completed cardio workouts. Gradually, my weight decreased, and my energy level increased. Since age fifty, I've completed four half marathons. We don't get guarantees on our health, but with my weight loss I improved the odds of staying healthier longer. Physically, I gave myself renewed energy and a chance to forge a new way. Eldo remembers when I began the regimen. "You became happier, more upbeat about life," he said. "I was worried about you before. You were down more often and had less interest in life in general."

I used discussions with family and friends to help guide my decisions. After Eldo's stroke, his physician referred him to a counselor. Luckily, he found a wise one, who asked thoughtful questions and listened to his values and interests.

"I want to learn to read," Eldo told him. I can imagine the counselor going through the protocol. *Don't judge. Remain open-minded. Look for options that might prove positive for the client.* The counselor likely questioned whether the goal was attainable but didn't immediately close the door. In a move that changed the world for both Eldo and me, the counselor pointed Eldo toward Project PAL. Eldo remembers asking Judy whether he should give PAL a shot.

She turned the question back on him. "What do you want to do?" she asked.

SIX
Blindfolds

Reporters like me pick up reputations for being annoying, pesky people who like to pry into the business of others. On such occasions, I sometimes say all I've ever been trained to do is ask questions. In those first months with Eldo, most questions were of the nonthreatening, introductory sort. Reporters call them softballs. Over time, my queries became bolder. After a few months, the reporter in me could not resist pressing for details. "Can you tell me how you've gone through life without reading?" I asked.

"It was like being blind," Eldo replied. Physically, he could see, of course, but just as people who are blind make deeper use of their other senses, Eldo compensated through other strengths, strategies, and skills. For instance, in the grocery store with Judy, Eldo could not read the labels but could deduce what was inside most of the products because of the images on the packaging.

Still, images alone left him short of details about much of what he was buying. If he had a specific question about something he needed to read, he asked Judy. Most of the time this arrangement worked fine; however, in later years, when his diabetes forced him to be more careful about the food he consumed, he called upon his basic reading skills to learn more about a food's ingredients and sugar content.

Eldo also compensated for his low reading at work. He drove a truck for a few years, as did another of my literacy students. Eldo told me that when he originally applied for his license, applicants could have a staff member read the questions to them as part of obtaining a "chauffeur's license."

In their truck-driving years, my students approached "total blindness" in terms of their reading aptitude. Neither could read a map or road signs. They might recognize names of communities or other common words along a route, but they weren't "reading" anything.

Restaurants were also tricky for Eldo. Naturally, he couldn't read the menu. If he was with Judy, she would read the selections and prices to him. Other times, he asked the server about the specials or to recommend items. By himself, he might just order a hamburger or something he knew he would like and could afford. Still another option: he listened to someone else order and ordered the same thing.

Eldo regularly compensated for his reading "blindness" through his partnership with Judy. Beyond the difference in their reading abilities, she and Eldo have different strengths, which over the years, they have used to their common advantage. Outgoing Eldo built on long-standing relationships and street savvy while Judy ran the household, handled the paperwork, and helped Eldo with tasks such as filling out job applications. Judy also worked outside the home, including a stint with the Secretary of State's office renewing driver's licenses and related tasks. She was the groundskeeper at the

Church of Latter Day Saints when I first met her. Then she worked in retail at Walmart in the apparel department until her own health issues escalated. As I write these words, Eldo tells me just about thirty percent of her heart is functioning. Sometimes she falls, but she hangs in there.

"I don't know what I would do without her," Eldo has told me. At another session over coffee, he lamented his hardships but then added, "As long as I've got Judy, I can get through the other stuff. We know how to make do."

The Eldo-Judy relationship began the day Judy rode along with her friend Ruth Ellen – Eldo's cousin – to an Ealy family gathering in Mattoon. Judy lived in Moline, about a four-hour drive from Eldo. During the visit at Grandma Ealy's house, where Judy was first exposed to big Ealy family meals, Judy considered Eldo personable and appealing. She recognized his work ethic and his sense of right and wrong. They delighted in simply talking with each other. "We just hit it off," Eldo says.

Judy and Eldo became friends, but maintaining a long-distance relationship was not easy. Regular visits by car were expensive and took too much time. Long-distance telephone calls were reserved for emergencies or short chats on weekends when rates were lower. Texting and email did not yet exist. With all that, little courtship took place. Once, Eldo had a friend drive him to Moline for a short visit. Judy returned to Mattoon for a few days. Those experiences were enough that when Eldo made his marriage proposal, Judy was ready with a yes, committing to a partnership that continues and grows.

At that time, Judy didn't know Eldo was a nonreader, but she said that wouldn't have made a difference. She loved him and knew he had plenty of other strengths. "I think Eldo is the first person I ever knew who couldn't read," she said. While perplexed as to why, it didn't change her feelings. It simply became an issue they had to deal with when reading and writing were necessities.

As a child, Judy's family moved eight times during her kindergarten through twelfth grade school years, so she had limited opportunity to make lasting friendships. With Eldo, she enjoyed settling in to one community, sharing the ups and downs of daily life, finding ways to create a family environment. Judy says Eldo helped "bring me out of my shell." She is a reserved, largely private person who takes pleasure in reading, creating a home, and looking out for her family – as well as the birds and squirrels that find the food she places in her yard. When her children were growing up, she found satisfaction helping with their activities and, later, working in retail.

In addition to being a caring and loving wife, Judy helped in another vital way: when Eldo decided to learn to read as an adult, she blessed the effort. That was a crucial, and often uncommon, piece of support.

I had an experience that I can compare with this "literary blindness." Years ago, my wife, Kathie, and I were one of five couples vacationing together in Mexico. We rented a van and a car for the week. On the way home from dinner one night, a local speeding car rear-ended the van. None of us were injured, and while the local driver sought medical treatment, she was walking, communicating, and appeared to be okay. Clearly to us, she was in the wrong – out of control and going too fast.

None of us were fluent in Spanish, but the police brought in a translator. The police and the translator freely communicated with one another, but their information to us was filtered through the translator. We were told that we needed to go to the local police station while the local driver was treated for her injuries. If she were okay, everything would be fine. If she were hospitalized with serious injuries, the translator told us that the driver of our van could be held in prison, regardless of a determination of fault. Further, they told us that the driver was the daughter of a prominent restaurant owner. This was underlined when a man in a suit, said to be the family attorney, showed up outside the police station.

There we were, the driver of our van seated in the police station with her husband, the rest of us waiting outside in support. We were playing by someone else's rules with little ability to communicate. In many ways, we were blind.

The feeling I had that night compares with my sense of how adult nonreaders feel every day. The difference between nonreaders and my group of non-Spanish-speaking friends is that our backs were to the wall for a single night, directly affecting only the final day of our vacation. And yet that unsettling, anxiety-filled incident continues to impact all ten of us. It will always occupy a place in our minds. Eldo and other low readers face this kind of frustration and anxiety year after year, decade after decade. After our incident, we flew home to a familiar language and rules we understand pretty well. Nonreaders don't have that escape.

Adult nonreaders, fighting this type of language barrier every day, are prisoners in their own community, always susceptible to discomfort and possible ridicule or dismissal. Even when they find creative ways to disguise their liability, they expend energy to survive in someone else's world, developing routines to normalize their situation, always wary of the potential of finding themselves in awkward and even dangerous positions. It's a double bind. Low reading levels limit nonreaders' ability to function effectively and increase the energy necessary for them to compensate for their limitation.

Most all of us have been taught things that we've later found out deserve further investigation. It's hard to believe now, but prior to meeting Eldo, I might have agreed that a grown man who hadn't learned to read was simply lazy. Now I know that Eldo wasn't lazy. To learn to read, he just needed the motivation and focused help he didn't receive in elementary school.

Sometimes I coach Eldo, deliberately or inadvertently, in matters beyond reading. After working together for many years, I experience his thinking as broader and his mind as more open to new ideas. For instance, Eldo used to think of business operators with even modest financial resources as uncaring and unapproachable. He felt they lived in a separate world that didn't include people like him. Eldo now says he appreciates the effort it takes to operate a business and sees the challenges business owners face working with customers, employees, and vendors.

Our relationship is reciprocal. Having had a front-row seat to Eldo's growth fuels my desire to expand my own world. After years of watching how others influence low readers, I, in turn, became more careful about whom I set up as an authority to influence my choices. For fitness, I chose to listen to a trainer. In writing this book, I needed direction on how to move from my journalistic approach to sustaining a longer narrative arc.

Seeing Eldo's growth helped me see how much better I could be if I identified and then engaged people to help. This approach of knocking on new doors and using other people's expertise was different than what I learned when I was young. For example, I sometimes heard at home and school *If it is to be, it's up to me* and *Be careful about whom you listen to.* That's not necessarily bad advice – I do want to be selective – but when this approach precludes me from working with or trusting others, it becomes counterproductive.

I grew up learning that I should be able to control life's circumstances and that if I fail, I should *try, try again,* without examining new ways to solve the problem. Such thinking may contribute to why some students don't learn to read in elementary school and why those who try as adults give up after a few sessions: they experience one or more occurrences of failure, aren't instructed how or why to change their strategy, and soon assume they will never succeed no matter how hard they try.

While I risk being let down or disappointed when I forge new relationships and put trust in someone I don't know, I gain appreciation for the opportunity to grow by taking risks. Working with Eldo was eye-opening in that it revealed to me a wider range of human experiences in Mattoon. Although he did not speak of it directly, I sensed there were days when Eldo was low on food, usually toward the end of a month. I had never experienced having to scramble to find enough to eat. Being able to help, to occasionally fill his gas tank or drive him to the emergency food center, reinforced how fortunate my own circumstances were and increased my sense of empathy.

As kids, many of us played "pin the tail on the donkey," "blind man's bluff," or similar games where we tried to function while blindfolded. In Eldo's world and in mine, the blindfolds were coming off.

SEVEN
A Framed Certificate

So this truck driver walks into a gas station. . . .

No, this isn't the beginning of a joke. Lost drivers once were such a regular occurrence at some stations that staff could easily distinguish between people arriving for fuel and a snack and those seeking directions. "What are you looking for?" clerks asked them before they uttered a word.

Pre-digital age, before we received turn-by-turn directions by simply plugging an address into a "smart" phone, most of us were geographically turned around at some point in our lives. Usually, we found a sympathetic person, like a restaurant server or gas station attendant, to point us toward our destination.

However, when a driver says to an attendant, "I need to get to the place where – I think it's the Williams Company – is putting up some modular homes," I wonder if she notices that he has omitted a street address and instead used names (the Williams Company) and identifiable landmarks (modular homes) to identify his destination. Will she know that this man cannot read? While she thinks she is helping one more lost driver, in actuality directions she writes down might be useless.

Eldo was one such driver. He drove a truck for a few years though he could not read a map or road signs. The map in Eldo's cab was just for show.

As a driver, Eldo delivered components of prefabricated houses to construction sites in a two-hundred-mile area in west central Illinois and eastern Iowa. The routes he traversed included two-lane roads between small, rural towns and interstates with their quick, dense signage. Their system worked something like this: The supervisor described how to reach construction sites, sometimes providing a sketch. Eldo then used his personal knowledge of the region, forging a map in his mind.

Some routes were familiar, places or areas where he had previously traveled. From the directions or previous experiences or both, he knew about how many miles it was to certain points and where he would make turns. He memorized key locations along the way. Seeing these landmarks confirmed if he was on the correct route and helped him frame clearer questions if he needed to ask directions.

When he drove in new territory, he mentally recorded the route as he passed through the countryside and small towns: a local diner, an elementary school, a handful of churches as well as post offices, libraries, and city halls. In making his way, Eldo scrutinized these familiar small-town components and memorized the particulars – a red brick versus a grey stone exterior, a yellow and blue jungle gym in a playground near a school.

Outside of town, Eldo noted details about the terrain – hills, rivers, prominent trees – as well as man-made landmarks such as bridges, farm houses, and barns. This gave him a near perfect sense of where he was on the route, in which direction he should proceed, and even the distance to his destination.

After Eldo had driven a route once, he had it memorized. Familiarly colored or shaped signs (do any of us actually read the word "stop" on a stop sign?) and highway signs on which he might recognize the name of a city or town helped further.

All this said, nonreading truck drivers still faced big problems when they encountered detours, new construction, or otherwise found themselves in unfamiliar territory. A long-distance phone call was expensive and required that they concoct a story about why they couldn't find their route. Somehow, though, when Eldo got in a jam, he found a way forward and made his destination. And as far as he knew, he made it without disclosing he couldn't read.

In listening to Eldo's stories, I reflected on how much of our ability to examine, memorize, and recall we've lost with the advent of maps, printed directions, electronic maps, and GPS systems. Eldo's truck-driving tales were among my first real-life accounts of nonreaders. The stories left me floored and impressed by their teller's creative solutions. Perhaps I was naïve, but I had no idea adults around me were encountering such hurdles. Soon, I would appreciate that Eldo had plenty of company.

Nonreaders have attained incredible achievements. Perhaps most outstanding is Tom Harken, a millionaire business owner who learned to read late in life having hid his illiteracy from other adults for decades. His story is captured in his book, *The Millionaire's Secret.* Another nonreader, John Corcoran, graduated from college and taught school, later writing the book *The Teacher Who Couldn't Read.*

Such financially successful nonreaders are the exceptions, though, and the shame associated with not being able to read only complicates the situation. One young woman in Project PAL who wanted to deepen her appreciation of art by improving her reading initially insisted on meeting in a car, afraid that by meeting at the library (even in a private room) she'd be seen and then recognized as a low reader. Similarly, a health care worker would only meet in her office with a closed door, making sure no one could hear what was going on inside.

"Until I began this program, I'm not sure I knew any people who couldn't read," my area representative, Debbie Haynes, had told me. As part of her job, she promoted the literacy program throughout the region, with the three-fold goal of encouraging people who needed help to participate, recruiting prospective tutors, and raising public awareness. She spoke at service clubs and community groups and delivered materials about the program to libraries, food centers, and senior centers.

Members of the public often asked Debbie, "Why do people go to such trouble to disguise their reading inability?" For some, being discovered could imperil their job or a relationship. Others hide their low reading to prevent being labeled *lazy* or *stupid*. Most nonreaders prefer the dilemma of keeping their secret to facing the repercussions (perceived and real) that might arise should their inability be exposed.

Just imagine the fun naysayers would have when they discovered an adult was learning to read. They could dismiss a fifty- or sixty-year-old man by asking "Why bother? If you couldn't learn to read in grade school, if you haven't learned in the last thirty years, what makes you think that you can now suddenly decode the English language?" A cynic might ask why anyone would believe that a twenty-something handyman with low reading skills could improve several grade levels. "Wouldn't the money used for these programs," they'd ask, "be better deployed to help children learn to read?"

For most of their lives, nonreaders have been described as dumb or lazy, sitting around waiting on their government check. As a journalism student at the University of Illinois, I learned to ask both open-ended and specific questions to challenge such critics. Yes, the world has all types of people, including lazy and unmotivated. It also has some waiting for another chance.

Perhaps the most damaging naysayers to adult students are family and friends. Their opinions carry weight. "What do you think you're doing trying to learn to read now?" they might say. "Why don't you spend time on something more productive?" Such critics can derail potential students before they ever get started. These detractors prefer to stick with the person they know rather than let that person step out. "You're fine just as you are," they might tell the nonreader, a backhanded compliment that keeps nonreaders in their place, not challenging anyone else's world.

Another potential set of detractors are people who determine public sector spending and the program staff who receive that funding. "Wouldn't it be better to use these resources to benefit children?" critics ask. "Kids would benefit far more from tutoring or mentoring than people who've already shown that reading is out of their reach." Yet Travis Spencer, a local pastor, notes that kids who attend youth sessions are in the church for an hour or two a week. Those children are influenced far more by their parents and home environment than by classes or services at church. Thus, one of the best ways to help children is by improving the lives of their parents.

In the 1990s, Project PAL hosted an end-of-year celebration at which students, tutors, and family members gathered for a chicken dinner. Typically, a community college leader offered encouraging remarks while area representatives provided heartening success stories with suggestions on how family and friends could support literacy students. A few years after Eldo started his literacy lessons, at just such a dinner, Project PAL awarded him a certificate of accomplishment. Eldo had reached several of his literacy goals, such as reading to his grandchildren and sharing an evening Bible verse.

Back home, Judy placed the certificate in a simple frame and hung it on the wall by their kitchen table. When Eldo and Judy sat down to eat, the certificate greeted them. When family stopped by, they saw Eldo's framed award. When Eldo was in school, he didn't collect gold stars, but this award helps to compensate for the times he was dismissed or overlooked as a child. Now, all those welcome in the Ealy house see this visible reminder about the dad, the grandpa, and the friend who was learning to read.

EIGHT
Project PAL

In 1984, Lake Land College Adult Volunteer Literacy Coordinator, Pat Hemmett, combined two $4,000 state grants to help create Project PAL, Partners in Adult Literacy. She then traveled the college's 4,000-square-mile district, visiting and reaching out to libraries while searching for part-time area representatives to promote the program in their communities. In 2008, after twenty-four years at the helm, Hemmett retired.

It was a short retirement. The college administration immediately asked Pat to return part time. She retained responsibility for Project PAL, leaving behind other duties within the adult education program.

From its modest beginning, the literacy initiative experienced solid growth and acceptance. Funded partly through the Illinois Secretary of State's office, the now well-established program still finds itself among many initiatives scraping for grants and other monies to serve easily overlooked adults who want another chance. Despite ongoing funding shortages, Pat Hemmett persists. She knows the value of teaching adults to read. Amid the turbulence of higher education funding priorities, she readily champions the cause.

While her goals are lofty, her office is not. Hemmett works in a modest cubicle in an open-air space that once was a Walmart retail floor. The building's front lobby shows the remains of what was a state unemployment office, since closed for lack of funding. The building is now home to a variety of workforce development programs, including adult education initiatives.

When I started tutoring in 1992, Pat was among my first connections. After meeting her for a cup of coffee and a chat, I would leave her office with fresh insights into the world of literacy – a world that has largely fallen off the public radar screen. Like many program administrators, Pat has witnessed funding declines and guideline changes while, at the same time, watching an increasing number of organizations compete for available monies. Yet she's adept with acquiring and analyzing concrete data she uses to write the grants. She's equally effective when she advocates for her program on Lake Land's campuses and within the broader community.

Community colleges like Lake Land commonly house adult education programs. From this home base, Hemmett and Lake Land partner with twenty-three public libraries in fourteen counties throughout the Lake Land district. District communities range from small towns with a few hundred residents to cities with twenty thousand population. Hemmett employs part-time area representatives to recruit and train tutors and to identify and evaluate students.

In the early years, Hemmett's biggest challenge was finding people like Eldo to give the program a chance. Project PAL can only serve students who walk through the door. With Project PAL's target audience unable to read, it is extra tough to market to them. Compounding this dilemma, many friends and sometimes even family of prospective Project PAL students don't know they can't read, or if they do know, they are supposed to stay quiet about it. This is why referrals from students within the program are crucial and why student success is the best promotion for the program. Mental health agencies and government programs such as Women, Infants, and Children (WIC) also make referrals, and occasionally a close family member convinces a loved one.

Hemmett's 2015 goal (before the prolonged Illinois state budget battle led to the program's suspension) was to pair ninety adults who had a reading level below ninth grade with tutors for private, one-on-one help. Since more than forty percent of adults nationally read at an elementary level, that would mean that more than 23,000 people between the ages of eighteen and sixty-four in the Lake Land district need help. Clearly, the majority of nonreaders and low readers are not taking formal steps to address their reading shortcoming. Pat Hemmett and other literacy professionals know – and are frustrated by the fact – that there are far more people who could benefit from these programs than are able to or interested in doing so.

A long-time representative in Project PAL recently told me that older nonreaders like Eldo still exist but aren't entering the program as often as they once did. Many don't believe that stronger reading skills can improve their lives, or they feel that the time and effort needed to advance their reading level isn't worth the struggle. Another probable reason is that nonreaders don't think they will benefit financially. Thus, they need a different motivation to get started. Also, these older adults were likely shamed, dismissed, or labeled as "unteachable" while in elementary school. Such an ingrained self-image is an enormous obstacle. That said, even younger people who would likely benefit from increased job opportunities if their reading improved are tricky for PAL staff to identify, motivate, and enroll.

The year I started tutoring, only a small percentage of people who could have benefited from Project PAL sought help. Should enrollment increase dramatically, finding enough tutors would be a demanding but, Hemmett thinks, doable task.

An illustration titled "Pathways to Literacy" in the tutor handbook emphasizes a core literacy principle. The top left features the words "Where Am I Now" and in the bottom right "My Literacy Goal." In between the words *now* and *goal* are the steps necessary for adults to fulfill their goal. Wisely, the sketch moves through a maze of jagged lines, some leading to dead ends. Not everyone succeeds in this program, and even successful literacy paths bobble along uneven routes.

In the 1990s, tutors initially evaluated Project PAL students through a "sort" test. Students looked at a page of basic words, identifying ones they knew. Determining the number of words in a student's vocabulary, a coordinator estimated what level of teaching materials would best serve the student. Today, the program uses a multifaceted assessment tool. For one approach to word recognition, students look at a picture, then identify from a list the words associated with the picture. For another, students fill in missing words in a sentence. From those enhanced assessments, representatives can better identify materials with which to engage, but not frustrate, a student.

Tutors work with their area reps to tailor plans that encourage a student's progress, assessing students periodically to adjust the plans as needed. Tutors also track the numbers of hours they meet with students, in part for grant application data. Project PAL also trains tutors to help students experience success early. Such success holds student interest and encourages them to return weekly.

Having experienced failure in their past, some adult learners are skeptical that they can succeed. These students might question whether tutors will take a sincere interest in their well-being. Other students, in a hurry to see results, are reluctant to dedicate enough time to the learning process. For these reasons, a successful start is essential.

Wisely, the training includes information about helping students beyond literacy tutoring. In addition to improving their reading, some Project PAL students receive help with their writing while others seek guidance for balancing a checkbook or with basic mathematics. Some low readers may need more assistance than a volunteer can provide, often regarding medical or financial issues. When students show up with a major personal, medical, or financial problem, tutors know it's unwise to step right into a reading lesson.

For literacy tutors, tackling students' personal issues comes with the territory. Recognizing and handling such matters strengthens the student and tutor. Ramona, a tutor who began working with low-reading adults in 1986, said it's difficult to identify students who will stay with it. Family, jobs, and home life often take precedence over literacy lessons.

"It's hard for students to break away to attend weekly tutoring," she said, "and when they leave the session, they are going right back to the same environment they are used to." In addition to prioritizing their tutoring session, in some cases students have trouble completing homework in between sessions. To succeed, students must make a time commitment to their literacy work. They also need to believe they can improve.

Along with many successes, Project PAL tutors must weather disappointments, some more heartbreaking than others. One such case took place a few years after I began volunteering with Project PAL. Debbie consulted with me about pairing a developmentally disabled student, whom I'll call Will, with Erica, a community college student interested in tutoring.

Questions about Will arose. Were he and Erica too close in age? Did it matter that he and Erica were different genders? Project PAL had not worked with developmentally disabled students before, so we wondered what other tutoring support he might need. It was new territory in multiple ways, both exciting and demanding. "It's great that we have a young woman interested in tutoring," I said, noting that most all the other tutors were retirees or older adults. In my thirties at the time, I was one of the "young" tutors.

"I'm no expert on working with developmentally disabled people," I told Debbie. "The fact that Will took the initiative is a great step. I think we should do all we can to make it work."

At the time, library construction temporarily moved my tutoring sessions with Eldo to an empty retail space at the Cross County Mall. It was public in that people in the corridors could see us sitting around a table yet private in that they couldn't hear our conversations.

"If we can arrange a time that works for us all, we could meet in the same room at the same time," I said. "The room is big enough that we each can have our own conversation. If Erica or Will has a question, they can ask Eldo or me, or we can talk before and after the sessions."

We didn't know what the chances were of Will making progress, but we had a workable arrangement in a safe, supportive environment. Best of all, Erica was a patient, understanding, and empathetic teacher.

For several months, Will made noticeable advancement during his weekly sessions, and we couldn't have been happier. At the end of each hour, Erica provided a highlight of the session, which gave Eldo and I a chance to "high five" Will and praise his effort and progress. When Will didn't totally focus on reading, she didn't get flustered. Taking small steps forward, just as Eldo and I had done a few years before, Will began recognizing familiar words and sounding out new ones. None of us knew how far this might go, but having a front-row seat to Will's progress was a treat for me, like seeing my daughter complete a gymnastics routine she'd practiced for weeks.

At age twenty, Will had one more year of high school left, as developmentally disabled students qualify for public school education until age twenty-one. I learned that Will's performance in class had improved as well. Hearing about his academic successes, I congratulated Will. "Put those gold-star results on your refrigerator," I suggested.

Despite our celebration of Will's progress, through the grapevine we learned that Will's friends weren't excited about his reading lessons. In fact, they discouraged them. Sad to say, Will eventually quit the tutoring sessions. His friends' influence was stronger than ours. Why? Will and his friends spent much more time together than he and Erica did. Also, Will and his friends had a history of mutual support, a social element important to all people but even more crucial to a young man with a cognitive disability.

That sense of accomplishment I felt earlier? Disappointment and uncertainty took its place. It was easy to rationalize that there wasn't much more that I or Erica could have done. Nonetheless, I'll always wonder where further tutoring would have led. Perhaps Will would have qualified for a wider range of jobs, earning more and engaging more deeply with his work. Perhaps he would have been more self-sufficient as he navigated stores, restaurants, and public transportation. Maybe he would have experienced delight in reading about new people or places.

What is clear is that when forced to choose between what was familiar and safe versus what was difficult and uncertain (even with its possibility of new and potentially life-changing skills), Will decided in favor of his friendships. It's understandable that he valued his friends' opinion. Once again, Will's choice underlines that whom we listen to shapes our future.

Those closest to us can be our biggest supporters or biggest obstacles on our path to positive change. Friends and family might try to limit us because they know (or think they know) our capabilities. Sometimes they discourage us from stretching our limits if the results push *them* to consider the choices *they* have made.

In another frustrating literacy story, Ramona helped a young man named Ben move up four reading levels – from fourth grade to eighth grade – a considerable achievement. Ben then made a poor decision that landed him in prison. Ramona is holding out hope that by contacting Ben in prison and encouraging him to resume their tutoring sessions upon release, he will continue his reading – and personal progress. Ben's account exemplifies one of those jagged lines depicted in the tutor training illustration. His experience may arrive at a dead end. Or it might become a big success story.

NINE
Grandpa Eldo

A jigsaw puzzle of Paris sits half-finished on a small table in Eldo and Judy's living room. Seated below Native American prints of the American Southwest, Judy spends hours on and off throughout the day matching pieces that become pictures of people and places, like this one that illuminates a vibrant urban scene from the French capital along the Seine. On the couch, Eldo reads to his youngest grandchildren, Lowell and Sydney. Lowell prefers books about cars while Sydney is partial to stories about pets and other animals.

While I've never observed Eldo's story times with his grandchildren firsthand, when I checked with Eldo, I heard the reports. Eldo was clearly pleased as he recalled how Lowell or Sydney pulled up next to "Grandpa" on the couch or sat on his lap. I like to imagine them listening carefully as he reads.

Eldo struggled with a few words, yet reading to his grandchildren was a huge step for him. Eldo wasn't able to read to his own kids. He knows he can't go back in time and change this, but for the most part he's at peace with it. "I felt bad about not reading to them, but they understood," he says now. Eldo's children knew he couldn't read, but it wasn't talked about. They didn't ask for his help with reading nor did they raise the issue around the dinner table. Eldo doesn't know for sure if reading to his youngest grandchildren will encourage their own reading or improve their success in school (although studies do suggest as much), but he is clearly delighted to see his youngest grandchildren respond to the book, ask questions, and share this intimate bonding time with him. It pumps light into his world in ways he didn't think possible pre-Project PAL.

"I want my family to be able to do better than I did," he says. "I want them to have opportunities and material things I didn't." Eldo's story time with his grandkids offers him a chance to appreciate language in ways he had once only dreamed of. And so in the living room on Moultrie Avenue, where Eldo spends much of his time, the door to next-generation opportunities cracks open a bit wider.

It's easy for me to place this original goal of Eldo's – reading to his grandchildren – in the "done" file. Not so easy is containing my emotion. I'm the supporting actor who sees the lead player fully connect with his audience, the teammate who passes the basketball to a player who hits the game-winning shot. "Yes," I shout to myself. "This worked for all of us." I get to share in the accomplishment yet happily remain in the background.

In the scope of the reading world, one person in one small town doesn't shake the system. Yet we can have a big impact in our little corner of the world. If more people stepped out and embraced these experiences of freely sharing time with someone on the other side of the tracks, I believe the world would be a better place. Being part of Eldo's world, having a small part in his journey, then hearing him describe the reading scene at his home – I wouldn't trade that for winning the lottery. On the outside, we treated the session where

Eldo told me about reading to his grandchildren like all the others. Inside, however, it was special.

By late 1996, Eldo's other early reading goals were coming along nicely, too. In our sessions, Eldo told me he now read from the Bible, often in the evening with Judy. He could read from Psalms or randomly select a passage. They shared these moments together as they always had, but now Eldo read rather than only listening.

Eldo had also joined the community of newspaper subscribers who look at a newspaper's obituaries first thing in the morning. (A common joke is that these readers check the obituaries to see if their name is listed. If not, they can move ahead with their day.) He scanned other parts of the newspaper, too, particularly the crime and arrests articles.

Even as his reading comprehension increased, Eldo still gathered information by stopping and chatting at places around town. He liked the junkyard, the auto salvage store, fast food restaurants, and neighborhood diners. When he picked up mail at his post office box, he ran into familiar faces. Some, including elected officials, may not have always been glad to see him as Eldo had no problem voicing his positions.

His conversations with mayors and city commissioners sometimes found a place in our tutoring sessions. The City Council elected in 2001 was the first in Mattoon history to employ a full-time administrator, similar to a city manager. Prior to that, commissioners, the equivalent of city council members, ran their own departments with guidance from the city clerk and other department heads. "Why do we elect these people and pay them a big salary to run the city if they're just going to hire someone else to do it?" Eldo would ask. I didn't usually share my point of view, but I thought he missed the value of elected leaders setting the policy, then hiring administrators to deal with the operational details.

Nationally, much bigger matters dominated public conversation. The September 11th terrorist attacks on the World Trade Center forever changed Americans' feelings of security and marked a significant moment in the presidency of George W. Bush. At that time, neither Eldo or I had ever been to New York City. We saw, though, how ordinary people's lives had been turned upside down by senseless destruction. We saw how people around the country, including from east central Illinois, rallied to support New Yorkers. Firefighters traveled to help, and many people donated money, bringing folks of divergent views and backgrounds together emotionally if not geographically.

The terrorist attacks and the new Bush presidency generated ongoing discussion in town, including between Eldo and me. Why did some people hate and target Americans? What was the proper role for the United States in the world? Did we offer too much foreign aid? Did we intervene too much militarily? Not enough? Eldo thought we should focus our financial resources here at home. "There are plenty of people who need the help here," he said.

As for me, while I hadn't traveled to other continents to witness things firsthand, I believed that we should take a broader view. We should address needs in our backyards and reach out too. It's not only humane: it also helps us be better, more informed people. Sharing our differing views, I hoped, opened both of our eyes to what we might have been missing.

Back in our tutoring world, Eldo had initially raised the possibility of completing his General Educational Development (GED) test, the test that marks the equivalent of a high school education. The Mattoon Area Adult Education Center along US Route 45 offered classes and a directed program to prepare students to pass the GED.

While Eldo's reading progress was admirable, I didn't believe he could pass the GED. His reading skills remained well below the required level, and he was missing academic grounding in science, mathematics, social studies, and writing. On a daily basis, Eldo benefited from his strong social capital, but such people skills couldn't compensate for what he had missed academically. Eldo's low reading level compounded his inability to absorb new academic material. On a pragmatic level, Eldo's persistent health and financial difficulties precluded him from mounting the monumental effort that would have been needed to pass the test, not to mention that taking tests ratcheted up his blood pressure.

This was my assessment after seven years, having spent an hour a week with Eldo. During a meeting in 1999, I noted that he hadn't raised the GED issue recently, but the tutor training in me called for revisiting and at times resetting goals.

"What do you think about the GED?" I asked. Our eyes connected. I tried not to show where I stood so as not to influence his answer. He took a moment to consider, then said, "I really would like to have a GED, but I don't think it's going to happen."

His statement was both a relief and disappointment to me. I was relieved because working toward unrealistic goals is a recipe for failure. I was disappointed because receiving his high school equivalency would have been an enormous achievement for Eldo and an inspiration for other adult learners. In our tutoring world, though, we would find a different adventure.

TEN
Speckled with Stars

"I can't believe," said Eldo, "some of the things in that book. I'm surprised it's even allowed on the shelf."

The book we were reading has been removed from libraries for its racial slurs regarding African Americans, Native Americans, and poor white Americans. It has also been taught in thousands of classrooms across the US. Written in the vernacular of the late 1800s, *The Adventures of Huckleberry Finn* is a classic coming-of-age story. For Eldo and me, *Huckleberry Finn* and other stories by Mark Twain provided the foundation for the middle of our twenty-four-year journey.

Huckleberry Finn arrived somewhat by chance. Our formal lessons had been getting stale, so I asked Eldo for ideas. None emerged. I probed him about his past, his interests. When he and Judy were younger, he told me, they'd visited Eldo's aunt and uncle in Hannibal, Missouri, the Mississippi River town home to the fictional Huck Finn. There, they had toured Twain-related attractions, including a cave complex that a Hannibal website touts as the "oldest and newest of show caves" (public caves) in the country. Eldo wanted to learn more about the Twain books.

Since *Huckleberry Finn* was well above Eldo's reading level, it was not in his standardized adult literacy curriculum. Still, we went for it. Reading *Huckleberry Finn* on his own would have been extremely frustrating for Eldo – its dialect and writing style are considered appropriate for tenth graders. For this reason, I started each session by reading a page or two myself. Next, Eldo would read a page, followed by a few more pages by me, then another by Eldo. Having the context of what came before helped Eldo navigate the tricky dialect and complicated sentence structure. If he got stuck, I offered assistance.

We used a 1971 vintage edition copy of *Huckleberry Finn* I found on an upper shelf in the young adult section of the Mattoon library. A blue-covered hardback, its pages showed age but weren't torn. I pulled it off the shelf when I arrived to tutor, then restocked it at the end of our hour. Not once in our years reading it was it checked out by someone else.

At the time, our sessions had moved upstairs to a small conference area just beyond the top of the staircase, with a view of the Methodist church across the street. Along with the view, this new spot offered us quiet and privacy – out of sight of the second-floor children's activities around the corner and away from the public computer and young adult reading areas.

We spent the first minutes of each session catching up on each other's lives, then we plunged into *Huck Finn*. Sometimes we let the book direct our conversation. For example, Eldo and I discussed Huck's family life and how Huck's interactions with the Widow Douglas, Miss Watson, and Pap Finn might apply to our own family situations. We talked about rivers, their role in commerce, and what life would be like if we worked on one. We shared stories about fishing (Eldo was a fisherman), our youthful adventures, taking chances, and getting both into and out of trouble.

Sometimes our discussions wandered into religion, the Civil War, or President Lincoln. Current events also crept into our conversation, particularly the Mattoon-based, federal criminal fraud case "Omega," which by 1999, I was covering for the *Journal Gazette*. This scheme bilked between ten and twenty million from people across the country. Many of the nineteen defendants were from the Mattoon area, so the case was high-profile. Despite this red-hot scandal, the core of our conversations were driven by Huck. During some sessions, we covered many pages, but just as often we read a small dose, then called it a day. "Those stories tell a lot," Eldo said, keen to the book's complexity.

We read *Huckleberry Finn* over multiple years, mixing in other, shorter books, but always returning to Huck and Jim. Having started our reading journey with the most basic words and pictures, we were now savoring a widely read book rich in meaning and interpreted by accomplished scholars. To go from the most basic adult readers to delighting in Mark Twain was an extraordinary accomplishment. Even better, I knew that neither of us would have enjoyed these books alone. Together, we had a blast.

We read other books by Mark Twain too, including *The Adventures of Tom Sawyer*, though not always cover to cover. Some days we read five pages. Other times, ten. When Eldo wasn't feeling well, we might read a couple pages and stop. Our reading rate, by most standards, was a snail's pace. For us, it was ideal.

Eldo told me he related to Huck, his stories, and the way Twain told them. Twain's dialogue made sense to Eldo, although he was surprised by some of Twain's language and attitudes, particularly those about race. This prompted a discussion about the time period and about how much, or how little, things had changed.

Periodically, we would place ourselves in a passage and discuss how we would feel in those circumstances. For example:

> Sometimes we'd have that whole river all to ourselves for the longest time. Yonder was the banks and the islands, across the water, and maybe a spark – which was a candle in a cabin window – and sometimes on the water you could see a spark or two – on a raft or a scow, you know; and maybe you could hear a fiddle or a song coming over from one of them crafts. It's lovely to live on a raft. We had the sky, up there, all speckled with stars, and we used to lay on our backs and look up at them, and discuss about whether they was made, or only just happened.

Where do stars come from? How would we experience life on a raft? How do we see the world differently than others?

The best decision I made as a tutor was exploring Huck's world with Eldo. I doubt that anyone spent so long on a single book. I also doubt any two adults experienced more gratification reading to each other or that anyone found more uses for a single title. Seventeen years later, those stories still arise in the conversations Eldo and I have. Eldo and I talked about taking a trip to Hannibal with our families, but we never followed through. Still, in our imaginations, we traveled not only to Hannibal but to 1840 as well.

When Eldo set his reading goals, he never mentioned wanting to read for pleasure. Yet here we were, reading and discussing one of the most celebrated novels in American literature. If I had to choose between helping Eldo attain his GED or helping him experience the larger world through Mark Twain and *The Adventures of Huckleberry Finn*, I would choose Huck every time.

ELEVEN
The Mayor of Moultrie Avenue

A few years ago, an urban-based writer referred to Mattoon as a "hardscrabble" Midwestern town, a reference that offended locals. The writer might have arrived at the description by driving through a neighborhood like Grant Park on Mattoon's northeast side. Some houses in Grant Park are in need of major repair, and many are priced less than a new automobile. Grant Park is also Eldo's home base.

In Eldo's youth, Grant Park was a happening place, anchored by neighborhood grocery stores, such as Weir's, where Eldo, as a teenager, helped stock shelves and sweep floors. Grant Park also sported a used car lot and nearby was a well-known local drive-in restaurant called Gill's, famous for its chili mac. Don't get me wrong. Grant Park was never a main commercial district, but the neighborhood once offered more than it does today. A few small businesses continue to operate in the area, but Grant Park is the part of town officials avoid when showing off Mattoon to visitors they want to impress.

In Eldo's youth, open lots in Grant Park hosted community events, including tent revivals for traveling preachers hoping to convert souls. Preachers stayed with local families, spending days and evenings in the neighborhood. The principles expressed in those revival sermons – *Love the Lord, Love Your Neighbor, Repent Sins,* and *Obey the Ten Commandments* – provided a basis for the beliefs of many Moultrie Avenue residents.

In 1983, as a first-year reporter, I lived in Grant Park. Single, right out of college, and earning $210 a week at the newspaper – not a bad wage at that time – I needed something modest in order to stay within my budget. My second-floor, two-room apartment was up an outdoor wooden staircase that separated me from street-level activities. Save for a television set, I had virtually nothing of value (unless someone liked to collect newspapers and reporters' notebooks), so I wasn't alarmed about neighborhood crime.

I now live on Country Club Road, a quarter mile from the driving range and clubhouse of the Mattoon Golf & Country Club. My home in the older section of this neighborhood is modest, built into a slight slope. Higher-end houses begin about a quarter mile away. In Mattoon, higher-end real estate starts around $250,000 for a few-thousand-square-foot home on a big lot.

I regularly drive through Grant Park, usually to see Eldo, but I also spent twelve years on the board of a local emergency food pantry there. The food pantry, where for many years Eldo volunteered for custodial duties, is among the newest structures in the neighborhood, a concrete base covered by a metal building. Before I knew Eldo, I didn't notice the dearth of sidewalks and curbs in the area. Now I notice every time. "Years ago we were promised sidewalks," Eldo has often told me. "They've all forgotten that now."

The question of sidewalks came up in our discussions about city government, past and present. Initially, Eldo and I avoided politics and religion, but as our relationship grew, so did our range of topics. Sometimes Eldo was bothered by an arrest or unsolved theft in the neighborhood. He felt that the police treated Grant Park crime differently than the rest of town.

On the other hand, he didn't like the nuisance officer poking around for cars without license plates in his or his neighbors' driveways. "They say they are understaffed, that they don't have enough officers," he says. "But they sure are around every time I want to fix up an old car and put it back on the street."

Eldo has been cited for nuisance violations. He sees nothing wrong with purchasing an old vehicle for little or no money – one that appeared to be on its last legs – parking it in the driveway, repairing it, and turning it into an affordable piece of transportation. "If the vehicle had no license plate for a period of time," he told me, "it didn't bother anyone other than the nuisance officer."

Grant Park attracts attention from City Hall in part because nearby ball fields host tournaments with teams from across Illinois. The city wants to put its best foot forward for visitors. Eldo and other Grant Park residents consider the "cleanup" efforts as harassment of people trying to make a go among difficult circumstances.

Except for a couple years in Moline at the beginning of in his married life, Eldo has made his home in Grant Park, mostly within a four-block area. For Eldo, growing up in Grant Park meant that people looked out for one another. Gregarious, curious, usually helpful, and seen by most as someone easy to talk with, Eldo has told me repeatedly that all he has ever known was how to help people. Clearly, the neighborhood spirit made a lasting impression.

Eldo keeps this tradition alive. In addition to fixing, then giving away push mowers, Eldo does odd jobs for people and doesn't charge a thing. Eldo once replaced a broken window for a woman in her eighties and told her that instead of paying him, she should help someone else when she had the opportunity. When we first met, Eldo mowed the grass for a neighbor, another older woman who couldn't get out of the house to do yard work. He didn't charge her anything.

"Why don't you at least recover your gas money?" I asked. "She appreciates what you do and she realizes that gas isn't free."

"She doesn't have much. She can't afford that," he replied.

"But you don't have extra money either," I countered. "If not for you, she would have to do something. You should at least recover your costs."

"No," Eldo repeated. "We need to look after people. If you help someone else, it will come back to you."

Judy sometimes says that Eldo would give away his last dollar. Often, that's about what he does. As part of his repair work, he looks in on people living alone. One day Eldo told me, "I got a call at three thirty this morning from a woman down the street because her toilet was running. So I got up and fixed it."

While some might describe Eldo as a loyal neighbor who displays Christian charity, others might say his poor business sense compounds his financial problems. For Eldo, though, generosity is the right way to treat people. That's how neighbors interacted back in his day, and he has no plans to change.

Here in the second decade of the twenty-first century, Eldo can be seen as an ardent environmentalist, working to reduce waste by salvaging and repairing items most of us would send to the junkyard. In fact, the junkyard is a regular stop on Eldo's travels in and around

Moultrie Avenue. He is skilled at finding old parts to help repair items others view as junk, such as Weed eaters, toasters, small drills, and lawnmowers, then matching them up with neighbors who need them.

Eldo has purchased automobiles for as little as one hundred dollars, repaired them, and sold them for a small profit. He erected a tent-like structure in his backyard to house tools and the knickknack stuff he had at any given moment. The structure was in part to discourage potential vandals and also to keep the city nuisance officer at bay. Vandals broke in anyway. While it bothers him that people take things, he doesn't let it get him down.

When Eldo delved into local politics, sometimes related to Grant Park, I found a way to encourage a smile. "You ought to run for the City Council," I told him. "I'll help you with your campaign." I couldn't have formally helped him while employed at the newspaper, of course, but it kept conversation interesting and light.

"No way," he countered. "I'm not smart enough to do that. I could never get elected." Other times he said, "They would have me in jail." In that comment, he was referring to former elected officials he liked who were heavily criticized when they tried to change work rules and past practices. In his view, these individuals were unduly criticized by establishment politicians, though not sent to jail.

When I, in turn, offered an opinion about a topic before the City Council, he deployed the same tactic. He'd chuckle, then say, "You ought to run for mayor. I'll help on your campaign."

I'd return the smile. "I am not interested in that. I'd never be elected, anyway. But thanks for thinking of me."

Even as I'd say it, I would be aware of the ease with which we now navigated our relationship. We talked about politics and exchanged lighthearted barbs and considered it routine. Like Huck and Jim on the raft, we found ways to "steer the course" within an unconventional system. On our journey, we merged unchartered territory of differing backgrounds into a liberating sense of discovery and common language.

Occasionally, Eldo, the careful listener as well as ardent storyteller, heard about local circumstances of international scope. In 2015, Eldo mentioned that the price paid for aluminum had dropped dramatically, half or more. The price for other scrap items potentially convertible into cash also plummeted.

"I was over at the salvage yard the other day, and the owner said he might close if it doesn't get better," Eldo told me.

My thought? "Is it really that bad? Is this a cyclical thing?"

A day later, one of the major stories in the US edition of *Financial Times*, a London-based newspaper, detailed how a slowing international economy led to depressed prices for aluminum and steel. Eldo and his network had delivered the news to me before the international press filled in the details. More importantly, if not for Eldo, I wouldn't have realized how this story was impacting those around me.

Eldo knew people in parts of town I rarely frequented. He heard about issues on the street before they arrived on the City Council or school board agenda. He helped me appreciate the community's pulse for controversial matters. For example, in December 2003, more than nine hundred people, including Eldo, attended a heated school board meeting that debated a proposed twenty percent increase in the local property tax levy. The meeting was in the gym of one of two new elementary schools, schools that were much needed in my view but rejected by voters. That the school board moved forward without voters left many people, including Eldo, feeling as if their opinions didn't count. At the tax levy hearing, the board approved the increase over objections from those in the audience. "Just another example of how it doesn't matter what those of us on Moultrie Avenue think," Eldo commented. "Board members will just do what they want."

Local politics breathe life into communities large and small. In Mattoon, one place to feel the pulse is at de Buhr's Feed and Seed. This more than one-hundred-year-old retail establishment is embedded within a series of longtime businesses in the 2000 block of Western Avenue. An east-west street that begins in the center of town and runs parallel to Moultrie Avenue, Western Avenue extends another twenty-three blocks to the city's western edge. The locally owned retail shops quickly turn into a residential corridor of older homes well protected by mature trees. It's a pleasant drive that passes Lytle Park, the home of the largest outdoor swimming pool in Illinois and, as of 2003, the modern Riddle Elementary School, one of those two new grade schools which residents voted against but were built anyway.

From 1983, when I arrived in town, until his death in 2012, Bernard de Buhr, Sr., was a fixture at the Feed and Seed store and in the community. Born in 1928 in an apartment above the store, de Buhr welcomed people from throughout Mattoon and the surrounding area to purchase everything from garden and landscape materials to pet food and a variety of salsas. De Buhr hauled the items from the checkout counter and placed them in customers' cars, some angle-parked in front of this wide section of Western, others parked at the back.

De Buhr readily discussed his customers' family matters and life events, along with sports results and the latest politics from City Hall, the school district office, and state and national government.

Hard-working and personable, de Buhr found conversation both easy and good for business. For this, Bernard de Buhr, Sr., was commonly known as "The Mayor of Western Avenue," a title he accepted so long as it remained honorary.

Moultrie Avenue runs the east-west length of Mattoon, including Eldo's home turf on the east end, beginning at First Street then running west to 18th Street, where it hits the Canadian National Railroad track before picking up again. The railroad, a north-south route, is a daily stop for Amtrak's train, "The City of New Orleans," the train featured in Steve Goodman's 1971 hit song of the same name. Before Grant Park was annexed into Mattoon's city limits, the county had placed a holding cell at the eastern edge of Grant Park for those awaiting transportation to the county jail eight miles further east in Charleston.

In his younger days, Eldo knew everyone in his neighborhood by name. He could tell you where they lived and worked, to whom they were related, and often, what daily concerns they faced, including who had been in that county jail cell the weekend before. Eldo didn't operate a retail store like the de Buhr family, but he and others in his neighborhood were and still are an efficient and expansive version of a "human Internet" for Grant Park births, deaths, and Little League scores.

Because he is so central to his community, I affectionately dubbed Eldo "The Mayor of Moultrie Avenue." The title comes only from me, but he's earned it.

TWELVE
If You Had Called from Chicago

In October 2014 in celebration of Eldo and Judy's fiftieth wedding anniversary, Kathie and I treated them to dinner at a local restaurant. Judy's choice was a locally owned roadhouse. It marked the first time our wives joined us. We couldn't have had a better evening. Our discussion, along with laughter, about children, family, and life in Mattoon, came easily. Because Kathie's father was a newspaper editor who grew up in neighboring Cumberland County and worked for a few years in Mattoon, Kathie knows most everyone in town along with many of the businesses that have appeared and disappeared over the years. When Kathie asked, "Do you remember the soda fountain at Kresge's? The Woolworth store downtown? Eating at the Dinner Bell?" Eldo provided details, always flavored with a story.

The dinner not only recognized their milestone anniversary but also exemplified the evolution of our relationship. Eldo and I had declared no specific date with a proclamation that read "Today, being friends means more than literacy lessons." Instead, our partnership grew and deepened day by day.

One evolutionary mark came in the late 1990s by way of a simple act of transportation. Eldo's home is just a few blocks diversion on my route from my office to the Mattoon Public Library. "Why don't I just swing by and pick you up next week?" I said one day. Eldo agreed. The arrangement gave us time to catch up on family developments on the five-minute drive to the library.

Usually that drive took us past the collection of ball fields two blocks from Eldo's home. The west end of the complex sported four diamonds for youth baseball. The east end held four softball diamonds. Across the street lay the field for Mattoon's junior football league; this field, in turn, leads to youth soccer and T-ball fields. The diamonds are constructed on what, in Eldo's youth, was the train depot for the Big Four railroad. The tracks and the industrial-type activity they spawned are long gone.

The youth ball fields also represent an area where Eldo's life and mine intersect, though in different time periods. Eldo was a youth league baseball coach when his children were young, as was I. Babe Ruth League is a time-honored summer tradition in Mattoon, which once billed itself as the baseball capital of the world because of the high percentage of youth league participation.

My children were just reaching school age when I met Eldo, so he and I tracked their exploits through many years. As for Eldo's children, all but one were out of high school when we began working together, so through Eldo's eyes, we shared the joys and heartaches of their young adult lives.

Regularly as the years went on, we updated each other about our children. I shared results of recent athletic events, "growing up" issues like a disagreement between friends, or scrapes acquired on the playground. Eldo observed his children raising their own kids, handling their finances, and weathering family conflicts. Sharing our experiences of fatherhood was one of our earliest bonding experiences.

From my standpoint, during the heartaches, Eldo was too hard on himself as a father. Likewise, he didn't fully recognize his influence on the joys. This became a theme for both of us. Occasionally, life's struggles caused Eldo to "dump" his woes as we drove to the library or at the beginning of our tutoring sessions, to vent for a minute or two – or maybe ten or fifteen – about his health and financial concerns. Yet he and I were committed to working through the hard times, keeping them in perspective, and setting up the chance to feel better and be more productive upon leaving our meeting. We also believed that as a stronger reader, Eldo was better able to ask questions about his health, take better care of himself, and ultimately feel better about himself.

Still, after I drove him home from a tutoring session, he'd sometimes say of his complaining, "My bullshit must get old to you."

"Not really," I would assure him. "You help open my eyes to pieces of the world I should better understand."

Before he walked to his front door, I usually asked him to think about something uplifting. He often mentioned his long-standing marriage with Judy. Other times he mentioned a work experience, his house, or a favorite memory.

"See," I said. "Don't overlook the positive parts of your life. Dwelling only on the problems isn't the answer." Nor was it good for his blood pressure.

"Thanks," he replied. "You are like a brother. I don't know what I would do without you."

Growing up as the youngest child with no brothers, I didn't relate to a blood brother as Eldo did. Still, our experiences resemble the way I picture brothers. We appreciated each other's company, encouraged each other during the "down" moments, and helped each other see things that otherwise might remain underground.

As for myself, Mr. Tutor, while I tried to avoid dumping on Eldo, at times I revealed that my life wasn't perfect either. Eldo became the sounding board for a frustrating moment at home or work. After one such outburst, as he was about to open the car door to return to his house, he asked me to think about something positive in my life, then let out a small laugh. He'd given me a dose of my own medicine.

We helped each other in more tangible ways, too. One day Kathie wanted a bush pulled out of the landscaping in front of our home. Within an hour, Eldo had a pickup truck and chain to remove it. He tuned up lawn mowers for both me and my daughter, Kelli.

Eldo was a master at combing used car lots. When Brody approached sixteen, I mentioned to Eldo that Brody would be in the market for a used vehicle. We hoped it would be one with substantial engine life remaining. Eldo found a Blazer we later bought. It was a dependable first car.

Whenever Eldo had a rummage sale to get rid of "stuff" around the house and generate some cash, sometimes I spent a half hour or so sitting in a lawn chair under the shade tree in the yard. Typical Eldo, he had a story for everyone who stopped by. And he readily dropped prices.

I have no physical skills to help Eldo. No one would want me to do anything mechanical. Yet when Eldo wanted to talk about his pile of frustrations, he would call and I would answer. This personal aspect of our relationship isn't part of the tutor handbook, and it certainly isn't required or expected. In the best of cases, though, tutors and students go the extra mile. In our case, that naturally moved into sharing each other's worlds.

At the end of a tutoring session, we often took a moment for reflection. A few times, our thoughts have involved tutoring. More often, though, we have exchanged a few words and a quiet moment. "I'll see you next week, my friend," I would say. "If you need anything before then, give me a call."

"I appreciate your friendship, Carl," Eldo would reply. "The same goes for you. If there is ever anything I can do you for you, just call."

While I appreciated his reply, I mostly took it as a formality. I saw myself as independent and self-reliant, the helper and not the "helped."

Yet in December 2013, I did need help. On an overcast December morning, I drove to Decatur, Illinois, where I picked up a company box truck. The air was cool but in an invigorating, not disagreeable way. As I headed northwest, I drove over the Kaskaskia River, passing cattle, horses, cemeteries, stately farmhouses, more than one iconic red barn, and thousands of acres of corn fields, now at rest after the fall harvest. I passed an Amish horse and buggy, clop-clopping along on the road's shoulder. Outside Sullivan I drove past a well-known senior living facility once run by the Masons.

In Decatur, a crew loaded more than twenty thousand advertising inserts to be distributed to other small newspapers in surrounding towns. Driving back through Mattoon, my first stop was in Paris, Illinois, well known for its basketball and a high-end restaurant out in the country. Then I was off for Arcola, once known as a broomcorn capital. Finally, I headed to Effingham, the crossroads of Interstates 57 and 70. The roads stayed clear, making it a pleasing day for a cold-weather drive. I had time to be alone with my thoughts yet appreciative of winter, the holiday season, and our biggest revenue season at the newspaper.

The deliveries were a success, moving pallets of inserts into production areas. At each stop, I had a few minutes to talk with fellow newspaper operators, whom I otherwise rarely saw. The printing press was gone in all these facilities. The single pallet I delivered occupied a small space in bigger production areas, now mostly vacant. The emptiness in most newspaper production areas generated a sadness we shared as industry veterans.

For the final leg of the journey, I simply needed to return the truck, just a matter of driving an empty vehicle another sixty miles, from Effingham to Decatur. Twenty-five miles from my destination, slowing as I drove through Sullivan – population 4,400 – the van sputtered and died. I pulled into a parking lot and called the Decatur transportation manager. He agreed to pick up the truck later – all I needed to do was lock the key inside.

But that left me in Sullivan and my car in Decatur. I was about to call Kathie when I remembered she was out of town, as were other friends. It was well into the afternoon by now, with few daylight hours remaining. Outside the air had grown chilly. I was thoroughly tired and, frankly, ready to get home to watch some football.

I needed someone to pick me up. I walked down the street to a Subway to pick up a bite to eat and to make one more call.

Eldo was there in thirty minutes. "Sorry I had to trouble you," I said, gratefully climbing into his pickup truck.

"If you had called from Chicago," he told me, "I would have borrowed money for the gas and been right there."

THIRTEEN
Twenty Paces Down the Hall

In 2002, while I was city editor at the *Journal Gazette,* Howard Publications, the privately held company that owned our paper (as well as fourteen other newspapers around the country) sold all of their papers to Lee Enterprises, a publicly traded, Iowa-based company headquartered in Davenport. Both companies owned newspapers across much of the United States. One of Lee's properties, the *Herald & Review,* was in Decatur, Illinois, a forty-five-mile drive along the two-lane Route 121. In previous years, we had considered it a competitor. The Decatur newspaper once had a news bureau based in downtown Mattoon, just a few blocks from the library. Now we would be part of the same organization. Perhaps more importantly, we would be part of a publicly traded company.

Bill Hamel, the former publisher who'd worked forty-five years at the *Journal Gazette,* told me the Howards largely gave him a free hand in running the newspaper. Once a year, Bill said, he had a business conversation with the senior Mr. Howard. Hamel's successor, Dave Simpson, enjoyed a similar relationship with the Howards. For sure, the Howards were interested in their investment in the Coles County newspaper operation, but aside from seeing the financial statement, they had little interest in the daily or even monthly details.

In the early part of this century, the national economic downturn and technology's upending of news consumption – the two most significant matters I would deal with in my career – were still a few years away. When Lee Enterprises purchased the *Journal Gazette*, my most significant immediate change as city editor was moving from a hands-off, private-company approach to being part of a company owned by stockholders. I attended meetings about how we might share content, engage in a joint project, and connect our newsrooms.

Within a matter of months of our purchase, Dave Simpson, the current *Journal Gazette* publisher, announced he would be leaving the paper for another job. As a boy, I had dreamed of owning or running my own newspaper, maybe a little weekly. Upon graduating from college, I had driven with two friends to Midwestern cities, scouting out possibilities for an alternative weekly. It was the perfect time, we thought, to go out on a limb. My friends and I chose not to test that limb, but periodically through the years I had eyed weekly newspapers for sale. Not being flush with cash, it would have been a stretch to find a feasible situation. Nothing came of my explorations.

The opportunity to be part of management, however, continued to appeal to me. I applied to make the leap from city editor to publisher. Technically, I wasn't qualified as I didn't have the financial, personnel, or sales background. However, I fit the profile for what our regional publisher sought – a person with a career in newspapers, with a community identity and openness to change. I was offered the job.

As publisher, my new responsibilities included participating in the sales process (which I was to learn from a seasoned advertising manager), handling personnel issues around the building (since I was a human resources novice, my boss and our HR department helped me through sticky issues there), and along with department heads, delving in production and distribution matters. Additionally, I was expected to engage in the community, take a leadership role, and connect with top people in the business and broader community. Integrating operations with our now-sister paper in Decatur, where my boss was the publisher, also consumed significant time. We moved production – the printing and assembling of the newspaper package for carriers – to Decatur, a consolidation that a few years later became increasingly commonplace in the industry.

Not surprisingly, I spent many late nights at the office. Just twenty paces away, the newsroom in which I had spent my entire career might as well have been in a whole other building. While this dramatic schedule change was a potential landmine to my tutoring with Eldo, at no time did I want to end our relationship. Eldo says he doesn't remember any significant change, but there must have been bleary-eyed days when I lacked focus.

Newspapers play key roles in a community's life – this has always been part of my attraction to them. I was drawn toward recording a community's history and engaging the people who lived and worked within it. As a reporter and editor, I had accepted the modest wages that came with such an appealing career. Now, though, as publisher, the financial opportunities were more attractive. Many others in the business community wouldn't be impressed, but to me the improvements in my financial package were significant. If the newspaper had a profitable year, I qualified for a bonus. If the stock price appreciated, I benefited.

Someone else found a financial opportunity in the newspaper business in those years: Eldo applied to be a newspaper carrier. His disability and less-than-adequate retirement income often fell short of paying his bills. When a medical issue arose suddenly or when his car broke down, his income could not meet his expenditures.

Since disability rules limited his earnings in the job market, as a carrier he was an independent contractor who, with reliable service and some initiative, could add subscribers and subsequently put more money in his pocket. Independent contractors are like small business owners, generating income and expenses. Knowing Eldo was applying for a carrier position, I maintained a professional distance.

A few times, our district managers contracted with him. He and Judy rose early, usually before four in the morning. Initially they handled a route in Mattoon. Later, after leaving the first route, they delivered a route in Windsor, about fifteen miles to the west.

Although Eldo was sometimes not physically up to a seven-day-a week commitment, he speaks well of his time as a newspaper carrier. I wasn't surprised that he tried to make it work. Nor was it surprising that eventually the daily grind became too much for him. For short periods, though, he had a little extra income that helped overcome the jagged edges of his financial world.

While our relationship would have worked had I been in some other profession, the newspaper became an important connecting thread. Eldo's generation grew up reading newspapers. Last I knew, he remains a subscriber, looking for the rubber band around the ink on paper on his front step each morning. He still goes to the obituaries first, then looks for other items that catch his eye.

Newspapers have long been important to me, too, though I've graduated to reading digital formats. I was hooked by my experience in my youth. In college, some weekends I would purchase two or three of the big Sunday newspapers, then scan others in the offices of *The Daily Illini*. I looked for newspapers wherever I traveled. Later, as a reporter, I thrived on the daily deadline. I relished the mix of writing and researching articles while knowing that I might need to jump to an unexpected breaking story. All in all, the newspaper life was a fulfilling adventure.

Learning and engaging in other areas of the newspaper business appealed to me, too. Before long, my schedule as publisher became more normal, leaving time for both my daily newspaper reading fix and my lessons from Mr. Common Sense.

FOURTEEN
Looking for Lincoln

The thermometer read zero degrees. Still in bed and half asleep, I received the first weather report of the day from Kathie. Mattoon public schools were closed, and she had an unexpected day off. Derick Fabert, WCIA-TV's weatherman, warned listeners of a dangerous sub-zero wind chill.

My feet hit the cold floor as I tumbled out of my warm bed. I showered, ate my bowl of cereal and a banana, then began the search for my boots, which rested in the hall closet most of the winter.

"Carl, where are you headed?" Kathie asked. "Were you asleep when I gave you the weather report?"

I told her I was planning to drive to Lincoln Log Cabin, a state historic site in Lerna, Illinois, about eight miles south of Charleston. Kathie, who typically errs on the side of patience and kindness, expressed her exasperation: "Couldn't this wait until another day?"

She was right, of course. I didn't have to go anywhere. Why was I doing this? Why was I being so stubborn? I had recently decided to widen my world and as part of that effort was following a suggestion in Julia Cameron's book *The Artist's Way* to visit places to see them in a new light and discover new insights. I was also following her suggestion to visit them alone. An "artist date," she called it.

The country roads leading to Lincoln Log Cabin were likely to be laced with black ice. Since local schools were closed, I realized it was also possible that a state historic site would be closed. Pulling open the living room curtains, we looked for the cars and trucks we would often see slide on the road as they attempted to navigate the curve in front of our house. There was little traffic on this day, however, most drivers giving in to the weather reports.

I called the historic site. To my surprise, someone answered. "Yes, we're open," a woman on the other end of the line told me. I confirmed my plans to go. I was no regular at Lincoln Log Cabin, but I was familiar with its offerings, such as a popular Fall Harvest Frolic where volunteers dressed in 1840s period clothing, cooked over a hearth, engaged in making dolls and other crafts, and served apple cider along with offering period entertainment and music.

Of course, with a temperature of zero degrees in January, today would be different. A thermos of coffee and a reporter's notebook in my bag, I buttoned and zipped my winter coat, slipped on a stocking cap and gloves. Outside, I saw my breath as my boots crunched against what was left of the snow. As I navigated the roads, I found it was cold, too cold for students to wait outside for a bus, but otherwise not hazardous. With little other traffic, I had no trouble on the county highway. Patches of snow and ice dotted the road, but there was no new accumulation.

On the drive, I thought about President Lincoln and what he, the myth and the man, meant for the citizens of Illinois. Like other Illinois school children, I was proud of the fact that I grew up in the Land of Lincoln. As a young boy, I learned to recognize Lincoln's unmistakable visage on the penny and five-dollar bill. As an eighth grader, my class made the obligatory trip to the state capital of Springfield with stops at Lincoln's home and tomb. On visits to Springfield as an adult, I passed by the Lincoln-Herndon law office on Sixth and Adams, where Lincoln once practiced law. Since opening in 2005, the Abraham Lincoln Presidential Library and Museum in Springfield has attracted scores of schoolchildren and thousands of visitors from around the world, all seeking a piece of authentic Lincoln lore.

I could have laughed or cried when I made the turn into the parking lot. Empty. I wondered if I had hallucinated the staff member who said the site was open today. Upon my arrival, however, an employee walked out the front door and turned the "CLOSED" sign to "OPEN." Around the corner, I saw a truck and other vehicles in the employee parking lot.

"You picked a great day to visit," a staffer told me, then disappeared into an office. He was being both playful and sarcastic. The greeter in the reception area looked up from her computer screen, perhaps thinking, "This must be the nut case who called this morning." She asked me to sign the visitor register, no doubt wanting verification that an Illinois citizen showed up on a day with a wind chill of minus fifteen.

She offered to show me the twelve-minute introductory film about the site, and I took a front-row seat in an auditorium with seating for forty to fifty people. The lights clicked off, and the narrator opened with, "Today you're going to step back in time to the year 1845 when the United States was a young and growing nation."

The two-room Lincoln cabin housed as many as eighteen people in the mid-1840s when President Abraham Lincoln's father, Thomas, and stepmother, Sarah Bush Lincoln, were subsistence farmers on the eighty-six-acre tract. I imagined eighteen people huddling around the fire on a day as cold as this one, inside this cabin made of hewn logs and lime mortar daubing and still not keeping the winter chill at bay.

I learned from the film that the future president periodically visited the farm and neighbors in the area when passing through as a circuit-riding lawyer. Some of his cases were in Charleston, which was one of seven cities to host one of the famous Lincoln-Douglas debates in 1858, when Lincoln opposed Stephen A. Douglas in a race for the United State Senate, two years prior to Lincoln's election as president.

In 2015, when Springfield and Illinois observed the 150th anniversary of Lincoln's funeral, I was one of hundreds who trekked to the Coles County Fairground to see a replica of the funeral train car that had attracted crowds on its journey from Washington, DC, to Springfield after Lincoln's assassination in 1865. I hadn't expected to be moved by the experience, but I was. The casket was open. I imagined how it would have felt standing by the tracks as the train made its way across the country to Illinois, the grief of the nation pouring forth at every stop.

This particular winter day what I most admired about Lincoln was how he put together a cabinet of differing viewpoints, including three people who ran against him in the 1860 election, as he led a nation divided by a Civil War. The brilliance of this move became the subject of historian Doris Kearns Goodwin's book *Team of Rivals: The Political Genius of Abraham Lincoln*.

Born in Kentucky, Lincoln's life and hardships are well documented in some fifteen thousand books. (More books have been written about Lincoln than anyone else except Jesus Christ.) Lincoln's life history is also peppered with stories and myths. For instance, how did Lincoln learn to read? The answer depends on whom you ask. According to Lincoln biographer David Herbert Donald, by the time young Abe left Kentucky at age seven he knew the alphabet. His father, Thomas Lincoln, and mother, Nancy Hanks Lincoln, were both nonreaders but nonetheless they ". . . had a sense that education was important." Lincoln briefly attended what at the time were known as an "A.B.C." schools in both Kentucky and Indiana.

If I could rewind the clock of history and overhear a late-night conversation between Thomas and Abe's stepmother, Sarah Bush Lincoln, about their son's education, what would I hear? If there had been a parent-teacher conference, what might the Lincolns have confided to – or asked of – Abe's teacher? What would be the ideal (or essential) curriculum from the point of view of parent-farmers in the 1810s?

Maybe this: Abe should learn to cipher and read. No more, no less – basic education. However, once he learned to read, what would he read and for what purpose? Books were a rare commodity on the frontier. Donald suggests there might have been only three books in the cabin where Abe grew up: the Bible that Sarah Bush Lincoln carried with her from Kentucky, *Aesop's Fables*, and *Pilgrim's Progress*.

By all accounts, Abraham Lincoln had an insatiable appetite for reading and learning. Dennis Hanks described Abe as "hungry" for books, "reading everything he could lay his hands on," carrying a book with him when he set out to work.

When Lincoln ended his formal education at fifteen, he had the equivalent of about one year of school. However, the self-educated Lincoln possessed something adult nonreaders need in spades if they are to turn the tables around and become readers – curiosity. Although curiosity is hard to describe, much less to quantify, literacy tutors, teachers, and coaches of all backgrounds know what curiosity looks and feels like in their students. I witnessed Eldo's curiosity in the way he absorbed *Huck Finn* and engaged with people in his neighborhood and throughout Mattoon. Unlocking the mystery of the written word, he opened previously closed doors, giving him the ability to touch – and be touched by – the hearts and minds of previous generations as well as contemporaries far beyond Mattoon.

By learning to read, Lincoln changed the course of his family history. His father, Thomas, was illiterate; he could sign his name but wrote little beyond that. It might be said that Thomas Lincoln was not a curious man, at least not in the area of what we might today call "self-improvement." While he did move his family from Kentucky to Indiana and then Illinois after losing three farms to boundary disputes, Thomas, unlike his neighbors the Sargent family, was not focused on self-advancement.

The Lincolns focused on raising enough food to survive, bartering with surplus for items they were unable to grow themselves. Meanwhile, the Sargents worked to increase their yields and profit from their work. By today's way of thinking, the Sargents were "upwardly mobile," and the Lincolns were poor, though there's no indication they saw themselves as such.

Driving home from Lincoln Log Cabin, I considered that seventy years after the Lincolns moved to Illinois, my mom grew up on a southeastern Illinois farm eighty miles from this historic site. Born in 1919, as a girl she helped her grandfather work the field with horses pulling the plow. They harvested wheat, lettuce, cabbage, peas, onions, green beans, tomatoes, beets, and sweet potatoes by hand. Mom and her siblings walked nearly two miles to and from the one-room Watson school, though Grandpa picked them up in the wagon on rainy days when Mom recalled huddling under a tarp for warmth with her siblings. Like the Lincolns, they would barter for items like sugar and flour when they visited the nearby towns of Johnsonville, Cisne, or Fairfield.

While my mother's older sister was assigned to indoor household chores, Mom worked with Grandpa in the barn, feeding chickens, horses, and pigs and slopping manure until her younger brother Noble was old enough to take on these tasks. Mom was probably reassigned to the kitchen when her brother came of age; she would have helped Gran keep the wood-burning stove lit or plan how to keep the family fed through winter. The principles and foundation for their life came from a small plot of land where they grew and prepared their food.

"We never considered ourselves poor," she once told me. "We had everything we needed. We worked hard, *and* we had fun with our friends. It was a good life." Mom told me that she and her siblings often took in a movie after they went to the general store in Cisne. They spent Sunday morning at the New Salem Methodist Church and Sunday afternoon visiting family, friends, and neighbors. Mom remembered Sunday as a special day of the week for children, bringing neighbors and family together for worship, play, and a common table, whether food was plentiful or not.

Fast forward to the 1940s, when my friend Eldo grew up on Moultrie Avenue in Mattoon. "We didn't have much, but we never went hungry," Eldo says of his childhood. If food was particularly low, Eldo, his father, or a neighbor would go to the woods and shoot a rabbit or squirrel for neighborhood stew. He remembers learning how to safely handle and shoot a gun by age twelve, sometimes spending a few hours a day in the woods looking to stir up game. "We weren't poor," Eldo emphasized. "We had what we needed."

Just as for the Lincolns and the Ealys, stability for my mother's family came from those around them. Neighbors pooled resources, always finding a way. Their genuine connection to one another allowed them to survive the toughest times. Eldo grew up in a world fueled by neighbors pulling together for their mutual benefit. Their focus was survival and relationships. Through his example in learning to read, he expanded that world – for himself and others who might follow his lead.

FIFTEEN
I Take My Coffee Black

Sixteen years into our tutoring sessions, I said to Eldo, "It's been awhile since we talked about our routine here. Let's take a few minutes today and think it through."

Periodically, as I was taught in tutor training, Eldo and I reserved time to review our work together. We celebrated his accomplishments, talked about my travels, his journeys around town, and how fortunate we were to have friends, family, and a generally supportive community.

Having had our fill of Mark Twain, our reading sessions had moved to short stories. We had found books on past presidents, cities, and historical events – the type of books other literacy students of mine had read. The stories wove together people and places my students knew of, some from events in their lifetime, others from history. When reading about South Carolina, for example, a section would cover Fort Sumter and the start of the Civil War. When reading about Massachusetts, we traveled in our imaginations to the beginning of the American Revolution. These texts encouraged further conversations related to present-day wars, presidents, and events. We had discussed local or state politics or how we'd like to see an economy with more jobs. We hadn't dwelt on national or international issues, though they came up, particularly since Eldo watched more than his share of cable news.

At the start of each session, we usually picked a book or topic for the day. In most cases, we had covered the entire book in one or two sessions. Academically, this hadn't advanced us toward higher reading levels, but at this stage in our work together, that kind of progress was secondary. The important thing for Eldo, who was now well into his sixties, was to enjoy reading.

Now, here in 2007, it was again time to assess. I asked him directly, "Do you want to keep going with tutoring?"

"No," he said. "I've had enough."

I wasn't surprised by his response. We had had a long and rewarding run in the reading world, and Eldo, who had begun with no reading skills, could now read menus, product labels, instructions, children's books, and Bible verses. He was still a "low reader" by external standards, but the names of towns on map were no longer foreign. I didn't sense he wanted to redouble efforts to go further, which would require returning to the academic approach to learn more challenging words and complex sentences. As always, his health was up and down, but now there were more days when he was tired, when the medicine took its toll, or when he just didn't have it in him to expend the effort.

My next question was the one that really mattered: "Outside of tutoring, do you want to keep meeting?"

A short but comfortable pause followed as he considered his response. "Carl, you've helped me in ways I couldn't imagine. Yes, I want to keep meeting."

My answer to the question was the same. Like Eldo, life obstacles abounded. My children were in or just graduating from college, forging new lives. My increasingly demanding job consumed more and more of my energy, sometimes in exasperating ways. But I didn't see our lessons as one more thing to fit in. On the contrary, I loved our time together. Now, with our shift from lessons to social time, I welcomed not having to review lesson materials or find something to read ahead of time. Even more, I welcomed the opportunity to spend time with Eldo in different settings.

Transitioning to a world beyond tutoring removed the Mattoon Public Library from our equation. While it was a convenient, quiet location that had served us well, we didn't need the library for social calls. Where to go next? For our next phase, Eldo was well prepared. In his daily life, he had a network of stops. He liked Arby's, Hardee's, and occasionally McDonald's, all places where he found the coffee affordable and the conversation engaging. At some stops, Eldo joined groups of curmudgeons who started the day solving personal, local, and global problems through groupthink.

By now, the United States president was Barack Obama, a former state and later US Senator from Illinois. As an obscure state senator, he had once given a speech at Lake Land Community College, the umbrella agency for Project PAL. A friend of mine recalls discussions at the college about the appropriate person to introduce state Senator Obama. Many people had never heard of him, so ironically, it wasn't a plum assignment. But since Lake Land was publicly funded, an appearance by any state senator required appropriate protocol.

Being a Chicago-based state senator, Obama didn't hold widespread favor in Mattoon, now or then. Many residents in central Illinois view the issues of urban life as far removed from their own interests. Illinois is heavily populated in the north in Chicagoland and to the west in suburban St. Louis, Missouri; otherwise, it is a countryside of some 57,915 square miles with a few mid-sized cities. The diverse concerns of such a state make for engaging fodder.

In 2007, US Senator Obama announced his presidential ambition on the steps of the old state capitol in Springfield, a ninety-minute drive from Mattoon. So Eldo and I spent time ruminating on the changes Senator Obama advocated. Eldo and his friends didn't like his views on immigration or guns. They felt he was too apologetic and should be more forceful around the world.

Along with debating the merits of the president, Eldo and his friends discussed the local economy. Eldo felt that the focus of city leaders should be in adding jobs. "They should appreciate and recognize job providers and look for ways to bring in more small businesses," he'd say.

"I know, I know," he'd sometimes add. "I'm sounding like a Republican." Eldo was a Democrat much of his life but in recent years, like many of us, had become increasingly frustrated with the political world.

The *Journal Gazette*, of course, was among the things discussed over coffee. When Eldo and I met, his colleagues were more than happy to suggest ways to improve the paper. This was helpful for me and probably them. At Arby's, we usually sat at a table for two. Before long, however, regulars who knew Eldo arrived, and the stories were on. We covered everything from harvest yields of the current corn and soybean crop to whether the City Council was correct to purchase property for a new public works building.

Except for meetings during our first two years, the confidential nature of tutoring a nonreader was a nonissue. We didn't make efforts to disguise our relationship nor did we go out of our way to boast about it. Were it to arise in conversation with family or friends, fine. If not, that was great too. Unless an acquaintance bumped into us at the library, few people saw us in action.

Life was different now. In fast food restaurants, we sat together. Usually I picked up Eldo, so we arrived and left in the same car, my silver 2007 Cadillac DTS.

"What brings you two together?" became an occasional question.

"We've been friends for years," I would say. "I worked with Eldo on his reading, and we've just stuck together. Now he teaches me all kinds of things."

This usually elicited a smile, satisfying the curiosity of those who considered us an unlikely pair – the newspaper publisher and his working-class friend. Or vice versa: the Mayor of Moultrie Avenue and his suit-clad friend. The conversation quickly moved in another direction.

I don't know how he does it, but Eldo befriends many of the employees behind the counter or working the grill. He knows about their families and often the intimate details of their lives, things like relationship problems, financial hardships, and the struggle to find a decent place to live. The workers call him by name, usually *Butch* as many know him. They make small talk, crack jokes, and create smiles on both sides of the conversation.

Eldo insists on a smile. If Eldo goes to the counter and a clerk he knows displays a negative attitude, he boldly says: "Make sure when you bring that coffee back you have a smile. Smiles are easy and you're too good to show that frown." Invariably, the smile emerges with the coffee. And the mutual respect for one another shines.

Eldo often reminded these young people that they needed to continue their educations. For most, he suggested they attend Lake Land Community College to enhance their skills in home health care, hospitality, technology, even his favorite: auto mechanics. On multiple occasions, he cornered store managers (whom he also knew), recommending someone for employment. When one of his acquaintances made a mistake, like getting in trouble with the law for theft, smoking marijuana, or engaging in a domestic dispute that became violent, Eldo might plead the person's case with a manager to give him another chance.

That led to discussions of "What in the world are we to do to find ways for people with criminal records to have any opportunity?" Just about every employer requires background checks. Criminal history – things like drug use or a misdemeanor battery charge – creates a red flag. "Are we going to mark them for life?" Eldo asked.

While Eldo knew most everyone in the restaurant, I, too, was a recognizable figure. Some knew me by name, others by position. The reverse was also true. Sometimes I recognized someone but couldn't place the name. Often, Eldo filled in the details on the person's life.

I continued to be as floored by the way he operated in these fast food restaurants as I had been by the way he struggled with the most basic words and sounds at our first lesson. His knowledge of people's names and personal history, his tendency to advise, and his willingness to advocate were all something to watch. More importantly, I was impressed by the influence he carried and the way he shone light where others saw only darkness. Some in my world saw only "societal drains" in troubled young adults. Eldo saw them as people with many challenges but also with opportunities to do better, if only they would keep trying.

Occasionally, I took Eldo out of his coffee comfort zone. Over the years, two senior coffees at Arby's or Hardee's ranged from $1.05 to $1.50. The diner down the street from Eldo's home was about double that. But there we sat in a more comfortable booth. So once a month or so when Eldo climbs into my car and asks where we should go that day, I suggest Common Grounds. That's the closest Mattoon comes to Starbucks. A single cup of coffee exceeds $2, though the refills are just fifty cents. Should I add a pastry to share, our bill might be seven dollars or more. He says nothing, but I can see his mind at work. "We used to scramble around the neighborhood and combine meager resources just to have enough for a pot of stew to share. And here I am watching someone pay this kind of money for two cups of coffee and a roll."

Oh, how our world changes.

SIXTEEN
Graduation Day

Despite a country club membership and my splurging of seven dollars for two coffees and a roll (a scone, actually), my financial values tend to the practical, even frugal, side. My parents taught me to be careful with money. I rarely splurge for anything flashy or luxurious. Nonetheless, in the fall of 2004 an advertisement caught my attention: a suburban Chicago golf association was sponsoring a weekend golf trip. The destination? The famed Pinehurst golf resort in the Sandhills of North Carolina. With crown greens, pot bunkers, and long-leafed pines among the features of nine eighteen-hole golf courses, Pinehurst is one of the world's most celebrated, and most beautiful, golf experiences.

In November 2004, I was past the initial flurry of activity associated with my appointment as publisher. And as publisher, I was receiving perks foreign to newspaper reporters – in particular, a bonus. Prior to 2004, I would have skipped right over the Pinehurst ad since I wouldn't have had the money. Even now, with the extra cash, I paused. While my parents, sisters, and I were fortunate to travel extensively while growing up, we covered the country pulling a simple camper behind our car. With my own family, we'd stepped up some. When traveling, Kathie, I, and our children stayed mostly in hotels, not campgrounds, eating hotel breakfasts and dining in restaurants rather than preparing our own meals. Although not as thrifty as those of my childhood, our trips allowed us to stay in hotels like Hampton Inns.

Pinehurst Resort is not modest. The cost for the three-day stay there was $2,500, an amount that, in the past, I would have termed exorbitant. However, as a lifelong golfer, I felt called to this opportunity. My play is run-of-the mill, a fifteen handicapper, so I appreciate hitting shots from the difficult positions where you're not supposed to hit a golf ball. I knew of Pinehurst's world-class reputation steeped in golf history. Pinehurst was where the late Payne Stewart made a legendary putt to win the 1999 United States Open.

For all these reasons, on Veterans Day weekend in 2004, I stepped out of my penny-wise comfort zone and into the world of five-star golf. On a Saturday morning, forty of us flew out of Chicago to Raleigh-Durham, where a charter bus awaited. We played golf Saturday, Sunday, and Monday. The two nights were booked in the stately Carolina Hotel. Dinners and buffet breakfasts were included, along with all transportation.

I appreciated the golf history that abounds at Pinehurst as well as the golf itself, including a round on the famed Pinehurst No. 2 course, where a statue of Stewart overlooks the 18th green. I'll never forget walking off the first tee with the required caddie, thinking how the greatest golfers to ever play, from Jack Nicklaus to Tiger Woods, had made this same path. The caddie helped me select the right club for the next shot, fueling conversation about how Pinehurst attracts and challenges both professionals and amateurs. Yes, it was an expensive weekend but, for me, worth every penny.

I had another world-class experience that year when my parents reached their fiftieth wedding anniversary milestone. With their cash reserve, they treated me, my sisters, and our families to a trip to Hawaii where we stayed on the Big Island, home to an active volcano. One day we kayaked across the Kealakekua Bay to the Captain Cook Monument, an extraordinary snorkeling location. Another day we trekked to the Pu'uhonua o Honaunau National Historical Park and took in a traditional (well, highly touristy!) luau.

My family took a plane to Oahu to see the memorial at Pearl Harbor and the famed Waikiki Beach. My sisters stayed on the Big Island with Mom and Dad. Normally Dad would have been in high gear to accompany us to Oahu, but he seemed strangely content to stay behind and relax. While in Hawaii, Dad fell, as he had on occasion during evening walks with Mom in Mattoon. Something was up, but we didn't know what.

In contrast to these travels, at this stage of his life, Eldo didn't take any trips. It wasn't a financial option as he struggled to pay his monthly bills, especially his health bills and his and Judy's costs for prescription medication.

On the longest trip of Eldo's life, at about age eighteen, the year he would have been a high school senior, he and some friends thought it would be fun to visit Florida. They scraped together cash for gas and food. Once in Florida, the car sustained irreparable damage, so they abandoned it. Hitchhiking wasn't legal then, Eldo told me, but they had to get home. They split up so they wouldn't be a big group, and in the evening they picked up rides. Cash depleted, they appreciated when a truck driver offered part of a sandwich along with a ride. "When I got home, I had a dollar in my pocket," he said. "I decided then I wasn't taking any more trips."

The bad experience made it easy for Eldo to dismiss travel outright. Besides, he didn't have extra money for travel nor did he have any particular places he wanted to see. The combination made it easy for him to be content staying in Coles County.

Eldo varied from that stance at times when he talked about how it would be fun to take Judy on a drive through Minnesota, where her sister lived, then on up through the Dakotas. They also talked about visiting Alaska. In the time I've known him, neither of those trips have happened.

Eldo encouraged my travels, however. At times, I can't help but wonder how some of us get more opportunities than others. Dumb luck? Our own initiative? In 2004, Eldo had outlived his prognosis by more than twelve years, although both he and Judy continued to experience significant health issues and, directly related to their medical expenses, oppressive debt.

I began one other endeavor that year. Earlier, I had decided that learning business theory and academic reasoning could make me a stronger manager and newspaper publisher. I consulted with my boss as to whether a Master of Business Administration degree might be valuable, and after receiving an encouraging yes, I embarked on a master's program through Nova Southeastern University. Technology permitted me to do most all the course work online. The student and teacher interaction, which was virtual rather than physical, certainly wasn't the one-on-one role I shared with Eldo. Still, I gained firsthand experience in the managerial issues I faced at work.

The master's program also put me in the role of being a student, learning from faculty around the country. Perhaps, I thought, my experience as a student would help me as a teacher. The teachers and other MBA students helped deepen my understanding of theories of human resource practices and marketing. As a student in online and hybrid learning environments, I met new challenges, including learning digital literacy skills. As I sat in front of my computer working on homework, I occasionally thought of what it would be like to sit across the table from my classmates and teachers at a coffee shop.

The experience opened my eyes to a more diverse world, too. While many small Midwestern towns like Mattoon remained ninety-five percent or more white, the rest of the country was an increasingly diverse mixture of backgrounds. When I went to the school's campus in Fort Lauderdale, Florida, to complete the program, I saw that not only was I easily the oldest student, which I expected, but also as a white male, I was a minority among the international group of about twenty-five students. I thought how much Eldo and I gained from each other coming from different backgrounds. Here was an opportunity to experience diversity in a new way. Were Eldo and I missing out on further opportunities through our isolation on the prairie? Or were we making the most of our opportunities by exploring the other side of the tracks?

Along with my studies, I soon discovered that having a front-row seat to Eldo's health demands now had a personal benefit. Those falls my father experienced in Hawaii weren't accidents. In 2004, he was diagnosed with Parkinson's disease, an illness which progressively saps physical and mental bodily functions.

When Dad first learned of his diagnosis, he was still capable of dressing and feeding himself. Over time, his motor skills declined to the point that he spent more than three years in a nursing facility before the disease took his heartbeat in 2011. My father – the competitive bridge player, the math teacher, the lover of athletic events – no longer engaged in any of that. He required help to walk from the lunch table to the couch, where he slept most of the afternoon. The television was on, but it was background noise to which he paid little attention. Not even a playoff game between the Cardinals and the Cubs in the ninth inning with bases loaded – had such a game occurred – could have roused his spirits.

I felt helpless. Nothing I did could help him regain his motor skills nor his ability to think like he once did. What I could do, however, was spend time with him, and that I did. Most every weekday, I stopped in to sit with him at lunch, helping him maneuver his knife, fork, and spoon. Fortunately, he always recognized me. We didn't say much, but he shared what he could. Small things, like a day when he remembered a funny story, became bigger things. One day after lunch, I wheeled Dad down the hall and helped him brush his teeth and use the restroom before I left him for an afternoon nap.

"Thank you," he said. "Who would have thought that you would be helping me with these tasks?"

The day we first moved my father from his house to the nursing home, my sister Lisa asked him if he understood all that was happening. In a normal, even soft voice, he replied: "Yes, this is my graduation day."

SEVENTEEN
The Power of One

"Who else," I asked Eldo periodically throughout our reading relationship, "might improve their lives if they could read better?" Sometimes in the library, other times in the coffee shop, still others sitting in the car parked on the gravel in front of Eldo's home, I queried Eldo about other potential students. Such conversations happened maybe three or four times in the course of a year. Eldo needed just a slight pause to consider. He grew up in a world with many nonreading friends, some of whom he still knew well from Moultrie Avenue. A few I knew of too.

"I've asked my friend George," Eldo told me several times during our early days of tutoring. "I've known him most all my life. He is a lot like me – never learned to read anything. Still doesn't. He lives just a few blocks away. He's got time."

"What does he say when you ask?"

"He says he's too old. I think he's just afraid to try. Or else he really doesn't believe it will make any difference."

Like Eldo, George has a family and close friends who know he doesn't read. For his entire life, they've seen him, perhaps helped him, disguise and creatively avoid his shortcoming. In my view, George didn't realize the impact learning to read would have on his life or the lives of family and friends. I didn't think he fully appreciated what he'd missed or the satisfaction he would derive from decoding words in basic, everyday situations. Understandably, since George and other nonreaders often experienced frustration or ridicule in school, George's fears that he still wouldn't be able to learn to read further compounded his hesitancy.

Despite George's reluctance, success stories like Eldo's are the best marketing tool for adult literacy programs. Eldo has both the connections and credibility to help others see the value of reading. For George, though, time ran out.

One day in 2002, George's name appeared in the obituaries that Eldo had learned to read. I spotted it, too, and expressed my sympathy to Eldo.

"George had health problems, and I thought this was probably coming," Eldo said. "Still, it's tough to see people you've known all your life pass. When you see your friends go, you know that your time is coming too."

"It's too bad," I said, "that he didn't follow your example and take a stab at Project PAL. I think he would have done well and that reading would have made his last years more fulfilling." Eldo agreed.

The world tells us to think big. The sentiment *Go Big or Go Home* appears on T-shirts, in conversations, and in books. Hollywood and the media praise the larger-than-life founders and directors of Facebook, Amazon, Google, Microsoft, and Apple. These people are worth learning from, yet the power of one, the influence we have and the support we can offer as one individual to other individuals, is sometimes lost in all the clamor over global giants. A single person like Eldo, like me, pushes forward with some new life initiative – in our case, reading together. Others see that. They may already know how to read, but perhaps inspired by our efforts, they consider a fresh perspective on a different life struggle or find some other activity, such as a healthier lifestyle or improved relationships at home, on which they can improve. When George died, I felt the personal loss for his family and friends like Eldo. I also mourned the lost opportunity of what could have been.

We see the power of one around us, both negatively and positively. In the newspaper world, subscribers often shared their opinions when they had an issue with the paper. Many times they had genuine concerns such as a missed or late delivery or questions about why an ad or article wasn't published the way they wanted. Other times, it seems, they just wanted to gripe. Even though I knew that some subscribers were just blowing off stream, as publisher, I took their grievances to heart.

In these dark moments of complaint at work, I called on the power of one. In my case, the one consisted of notes from those who took time to acknowledge something favorable about the newspaper. I kept a variety of notes through the years with messages like "I don't know what I would do if I didn't have my paper in the morning," "You are blessed with a command of words and ideas," "Your newspaper's support of the Jefferson Awards, and your personal leadership in their promotion, is sincerely appreciated." Or this one: "You have worked so hard and it really shows."

Yes, the issue of the day demands attention, and people deserve to be heard and have their concerns addressed. But criticism is just a part of the equation. We need positive reminders to keep things in balance, like those notes in my desk drawer that help me see a broader picture.

Spending time with Eldo, I became increasingly aware of the power of one, as receiver and giver. I remembered a time in high school when an acquaintance asked me to chaperone a local Special Olympian. The athlete had qualified to compete at the state competition at Illinois State University in Normal, about 120 miles from my hometown of Newton. They needed a man to stay with this youth in the dormitory and accompany him around campus.

I said yes. Years later, I remembered the overall experience favorably, but I didn't have clear memories of the Special Olympian himself. Then as a young reporter, I covered graduation ceremonies for a school in Mattoon that served developmentally disabled students. I didn't realize that the young man I chaperoned was in the graduation program. He spotted and recognized me. He called me by name as he walked by after the ceremony. I was floored to learn that what seemed like a small gesture to me played large for the recipient.

Sometimes, the "one" is something tangible, though not necessarily expensive. Eldo periodically mentioned the certificate he received at the Project PAL banquet, a visual reminder that some entity, in this case a literacy program, recognized and acknowledged his efforts. In one world, Eldo's, it says something about what happens when one person goes beyond his everyday world.

EIGHTEEN
Sweat and Tears

Prior to the recession that officially started in December 2007, my career path was certain: the newspaper world. I loved reporting, enjoyed editing, and took pride in publishing. True, as publisher, I missed my writing roots – life in the newsroom, the unpredictability of a breaking news story, and a front-row seat to lives of fascinating people and local politics – but overall life was satisfying. Publishing a daily newspaper continued to be a joy for me. Most everything I did with coworkers, with customers, and in the community I found rewarding. I even sang in the office, to the dismay of some.

Yet the 2007 recession that rocked the international economy, the one that the National Bureau of Economic Research says ended in June 2009, never stopped in the newspaper business. This wasn't a surprise. I'd read the industry's obituary in trade publications, substantiating what I already knew firsthand. Subscriptions and print advertising fell during the recession and never recovered. Increasingly, people were reading their news online. The big three categories for the Classified section – Help Wanted, Automotive, and Real Estate – all were shifting to digital. Some national sites, like Craigslist, listed items at no cost to sellers. Many young adults like my children received their news in electronic and fragmented ways, unlike my parents, who not only read the majority of their local newspaper daily but even read it pretty much the same time each day.

When revenue declined, the *Journal Gazette* adapted by reducing costs. We closed our office in Charleston, moved from two editions to one, and most painful for me, cut staff on multiple occasions. Later, we sold our building at 100 Broadway Avenue, which had opened in 1972, to the Lutheran church across the street. They planned to develop the building into a grade school. At the same time, we moved increasingly to digital platforms. It was the right move, but one that also took precious resources, including staff time.

Some days I felt as if the oxygen were being sucked out of newspapers, especially when we downsized staff. Even as this troubled me, I remembered the admonition *Don't let them see you sweat.* Publicly, I did my best to remain upbeat, to not outwardly "sweat," but as I looked ahead in those first years of the 2010s, I envisioned more cost-cutting initiatives, more layoffs, and more requests of people to do more for the same pay. I still loved the newspaper business, but for the first time, I wondered whether I should find another way to pay my bills.

I was in my early fifties. Could I survive another fifteen years in the newspaper business? Did I want to? The first answer was *maybe.* The second: *no.* I yearned to find something else, but what?

For nearly twenty years, I had watched in admiration as Eldo balanced survival issues on a scale I'd never experienced or imagined.

For instance, I had never questioned where I would find my next meal nor had I needed to sell a refurbished mower or floor lamp to pay for medicine. My concerns seemed mild next to his, though mine were just as real. I had regular bills to pay, including a mortgage and college tuition for my children.

While I tried to remain optimistic about my work during my visits with Eldo, I couldn't fool him. He didn't pry. He didn't have to. He was too good an observer to not notice that sometimes during our meetings, my eyes flickered open and shut. He could see that I was exhausted by work's mental and physical demands – the long days, the financial worries, the continual downsizing needed to keep the newspaper going.

I thought about Eldo and how, as he approached age fifty, he too had faced a major dilemma. That was just after his near-fatal stroke that had forced him out of the physical labor that had defined much of his life. He could have sat back and bemoaned the hand he was dealt. Instead, he chose to adapt and learn something new: how to read.

The challenges I faced paled in comparison. Yes, by 2011 I wasn't financially able to fly to Pinehurst for another long weekend of golf, but I still had plenty of time and money to play golf, dine out, and travel. Nonetheless, fulfilling, meaningful work was crucial to me – I needed it to be more than something to simply pay the bills. My gut told me that it was time to seek a different direction.

I didn't consult Eldo along the way. But I remembered his path to literacy – his early years and nervous first steps, shaky like an infant learning to walk. *Hang in there, keep going,* I encouraged him, and before long his footing solidified. *Keep going,* I now told myself, *and exciting things never imagined will emerge.* It remains to be seen if I can make this change work for myself as well as Eldo did.

He stands as a motivating example. So does his quiet, nonjudgmental way of handling my last years at the paper, when I increasingly struggled with the requirements of the work and began to mentally transition out of my job. When I let my irritability slip, he might say, "You know, you ought to think about some of the positive things you have going for you." I wonder where he came up with that line.

He was right, of course. When I reflected on my life, I reminded myself that I, like Eldo, was grateful for my long and healthy marriage. My job, as tough as it was some days, allowed me to leave at lunch and spend an hour with my father during his three years in the nursing home. Most jobs don't grant their employees such flexibility. My position as publisher, together with Kathie's teaching, saw both my children graduate from college. Shortly after, we watched them find jobs in a tight job market and pay their own bills. All parents know how wonderful that feels.

If I needed a reminder to count my blessings, I needed only to think of a lunch at the nursing home. I saw the best of humanity in many of the workers and the most heartbreaking in some of the patients. Occasionally, I could find both with a dose of humor. One day, a particularly dedicated employee was going above and beyond to encourage a woman with Alzheimer's to eat. "Just take one bite," she said. The woman wouldn't take a bite no matter how many ways the aide tried. Finally, the patient looked up and said, "Why don't you just take it?" covering the aide's shirt with lunch. The woman momentarily froze as she absorbed what just happened, then calmly cleaned up the mess and changed shirts. I admired the way this caring employee handled a moment in which she easily could have overreacted. That episode reminded me to keep things in perspective, not to take myself too seriously, and to appreciate the humor in everyday life.

In March 2011, the toll from Parkinson's finally took Dad's life. Alongside the sadness and grief, there was much to celebrate. Along with being a dedicated father, math teacher, and bridge player, Dad was an active community member. He'd been on the front end of supporting girls playing competitive sports and had helped start a golf course in Newton. Over his decades of teaching, he'd colorfully helped and entertained many students, including standing on his head when he deemed it necessary. Several of his students told me that to make a point while teaching algebra, he sometimes detected it wasn't resonating. "What do I have to do, stand on my head?" he might say. Occasionally, he would do just that.

While it's always painful to lose a parent, my family witnessed how my father was embracing life less and less. By the time of his death, his activities had become limited with far fewer things for him to take pleasure in. Fortunately, he still liked to eat, particularly sweets, adding a scoop of ice cream to his meals when possible.

With the passing of my father, Eldo and I talked more about parents. His mother had died when Eldo was just fifteen. That's when he formally left school, turning most all his attention to helping the household. Eldo described his relationship with his father as rocky at times, though better in later years. The demands of helping his family financially during his adolescence, when he wanted to indulge in typical teenage exuberance, caused friction in the household.

Eldo hadn't experienced the mix of work and play that I had during my teenage years. I worked some in the summer, helping a teacher friend build his house and also umpiring Little League baseball. I had time and energy to engage in competitive athletics, to play ping-pong at a friend's house for hours and hours on Sunday evenings, and sometimes to simply come home late and sleep in.

Eldo lived his adult life without his mother and lost his father well into his adult years. For me, in my early fifties, the loss was fresh. So here again, the reading teacher received life coaching from his star pupil.

"Sometimes I think of my father out of the clear blue, for no apparent reason," Eldo told me. "I didn't always see eye to eye with my dad. As a father myself, though, I began to appreciate the sacrifices he made on my behalf."

Eldo also offered this: "Once he was gone, I found that I missed his advice, that I missed *him*, much more than I expected."

NINETEEN
A Piece of This

I n mid-May of 2014, Eldo's number appeared on my cell phone. A call usually meant he wanted to schedule or reschedule an appointment. Sometimes, he called to ask a question or get advice. Not this time. Eldo was calling, clearly pleased, to say that his grandson Lowell was graduating from Lake Land Community College on Friday. On the following Sunday afternoon, Lowell's parents were hosting a graduation party. "Family and friends are getting together at the community center over in Windsor," he said. "You and Kathie are welcome to stop by."

Around this same time, my daughter, Kelli, my son, Brody, and Kathie were finishing their academic years – Kelli as a special education teacher in St. Louis, Brody as a high school social studies teacher in Pleasant Plains near Springfield, Illinois, and Kathie as an assistant in a special education class at Mattoon High School.

I felt fulfilled, and Eldo's call made life even richer. Through our shared experience, perhaps we had a small stake in Lowell's accomplishment. Emotion isn't a strong point for me, but I can feel a sense of satisfaction just sitting here writing this nearly eight months later. Staying together over all these years allowed Eldo and me an opportunity to share a special moment with his grandson.

Kathie and I had one other graduation party that afternoon, so by the time we drove the sixteen miles to Windsor, the cake had been cut and congratulatory cards were accumulating. I had labored longer than usual at the Hallmark card section of Walgreens for the card I chose for Lowell. I'm usually the one to rush in or to let Kathie purchase the cards, but this one was different. When Eldo and I started this journey together, Lowell was taking his first steps. Through Eldo, I followed Lowell's progress, including his academic success. Now Lowell was the first college graduate in Eldo's family.

Eldo qualified as a proud grandfather. Having seen firsthand hardships aplenty in Eldo's life, it was a real treat to watch him brighten, smile, and talk with favor about Lowell and his other grandchildren. His happiness that day countered some of the tougher moments, providing an outlet of hope for the future.

After a satisfying visit with Eldo, Judy, and some others in the family, I shook Lowell's hand. "Congratulations. This is a very cool milestone. Keep it going," I told him, "and best of luck." We talked more about beginning work, his opportunities ahead, and the upcoming stock car racing season.

Many people have earned associate's degrees from a community college. For me, this one degree will always stand out. The Ealy family and friends' support and pride in Lowell's accomplishment shone strong. When Eldo was Lowell's age, he saw job opportunities. Those same opportunities don't exist in Lowell's world without the training and technical skill acquired in community college. Eldo understood that. I believe Eldo's example played a part in Lowell's academic achievement. If so, that would mean I had a small, supporting role, too.

Lowell completed a curriculum that trained technicians to work on John Deere equipment. This work, I thought, would be a fine complement to his passion for racing stock cars. He also likes working on their engines, just like his grandfather and great-grandfather. As I turned to leave, I saw a plaque out of the corner of my eye – a certificate of accomplishment with Lowell's name on it next to the John Deere logo. I looked over and saw Eldo. That small role he had played in Lowell's success? I hope he felt it again.

"How about that, Carl?" asked Eldo.

"You, my friend, have a piece of this," I said to him.

As Kathie and I were saying our good-byes, Judy called us "friends of Butch and I." In my life, I encourage friends like Eldo to take in and appreciate the rewarding moments. They help cover the hardship. This was certainly one of those moments.

Kathie tugged on my hand. It was time to go.

Seven months later, I stood in line to pick up a sandwich tray at County Market, a regional grocery chain. Christmas was next week, and the Ealy clan was celebrating early. Providing the sandwich tray marked my gift to Eldo as his family converged on the Moultrie Avenue residence. Earlier that week, Eldo had invited me to join the gathering. I was looking forward to it.

County Market bustled as families put the final touches on their holiday food preparation. I'd ordered my tray in advance, more planning than I sometimes do, and it made for an easy pickup that helped me quickly navigate the holiday chaos.

Arriving at Eldo and Judy's, I added my platter of sandwiches to the other offerings. Family members brought side dishes and drinks. Judy had prepared desserts in her kitchen. For Eldo, robust family gatherings and holiday traditions go way back.

From the kitchen, where we squeezed around the table, I could see Eldo's living room with its couch and souvenir piece Eldo made at the foundry, a mold shaped like a dog. I pictured Eldo, years earlier, sitting on that couch, reading to his now-grown grandchildren. As we shared the holiday meal, I gazed at Eldo's Project PAL certificate, still hung on the wall.

Three generations of Ealys filled the house, ranging from their late teens to Eldo's seventy-three years. I listened as Eldo's son-in-law described a new business venture in which he saw potential. Daughter Patty talked about working at Walmart, in this, the busiest of seasons. Eldo's son John had a retail job at Rural King, a large regional retailer headquartered in Mattoon that sells a wide variety of merchandise, including pet food, clothing, detergents, guns, furnishings, and tires.

In our twenty-four years of working and socializing together, I had periodically met members of Eldo's family, including his sons Tim and Joey. This Christmas dinner was my introduction to other family friends and family members whom Eldo had described over the years. Now I had faces to place with names.

Compared to many holiday gatherings, one thing was missing from the Ealy celebration: there was no gift exchange. Eldo and Judy simply were not in a financial position to shower gifts upon their family. Their family understood. They knew the gifts came in other, subtler ways. Rather, the Ealy family spent the afternoon sharing the news of their daily lives – a story from work, a grandchild's achievement, perhaps a new health concern. For my part, the biggest gift was to share a meal and a little time with those closest to Eldo.

A few weeks later, Eldo told me how glad his family was to meet me. The gathering had reminded him of earlier Christmases when families shared each other's company and socialized without using Facebook or text messages. "This year," he told me, "the conversation, connection, and camaraderie were the best they've ever been."

As he said this, I remembered leaving Eldo's home that afternoon, walking back out into the lawn frozen from the winter cold, catching the last of the low afternoon sun. Standing there on Moultrie Avenue, I thought how Eldo had lived most all his life within a three-block section of this street. Here, in his eighth decade, the simple Christmases of his childhood – their emphasis on family, sharing a meal, and looking out for one and another – continued to live on.

That Christmas was exceptional for another reason: it was my first without both my parents. My mother had died in June. She had gone to bed as normal one Sunday night, but when Laurie, the woman who helped my mother with household chores, arrived on Monday morning, she found the front door locked. Laurie called me. Ten minutes later, I found my mother in bed, unresponsive. She died at two o'clock the following morning at Sarah Bush Lincoln hospital. It was a sudden turn for someone whose doctor had recently described her as his healthiest ninety-three-year-old patient.

With the passing of my mother, my role as her primary family support person was over. No longer would I be dropping by daily, taking her to doctor's appointments, and providing a listening ear. As the months went on, with this change in my life, I decided it was time to take on a project that had been lingering in the back of my mind for a few years: writing the story of my friendship with Eldo.

Two weeks after Eldo and Judy's Christmas party, my own extended family gathered on the Gulf Coast of Florida. It was the first time we'd all been together since our mother's passing. I set aside one day there, a day when everyone else explored the Harry Potter theme park, to sit down with my sister Candace to talk with her about how to shape my experiences with Eldo into a story.

Sitting on the front porch of our vacation rental, I pulled out my yellow legal pad upon which I had scrawled notes for this book. Wearing shorts and a shirt with rolled-up sleeves – a far cry from my usual clothes for this time of year – I talked with Candace about my early years with Eldo and the transformations he and I had experienced together. Taking in the warm breeze from the Gulf, I recalled my farewell party just a month before. Colleagues at the *Journal Gazette* had invited community members and friends to stop by, have a piece of cake, and wish me well as I left the newspaper business.

Professionally, newspapers were all I knew. The first time I saw a press run, producing an article with my name at the top, I was hooked. Despite the appreciation I felt for experiencing the industry at every level, I knew that I'd had a great run and that it was now time to move on and explore new opportunities. It was a bit scary. Still is.

I remembered Eldo's insightful comment when I shared the news of my leaving the *Journal Gazette* with him over coffee: "I didn't think you would last another six months." When he said this, only half-jokingly, I didn't know if he meant "last at the job" or "last physically" – perhaps he thought I might just keel over lifeless. Fortunately, I hadn't collapsed from frustration or despair but instead had begun a new professional chapter.

Many guests at the party had asked what was next for me. "I'm keeping doors open," I said. "I'm going to do some writing, some freelance work." Since my departure from the paper, I've written profiles for an agricultural journal and an article for a public policy magazine on the plight of local grocery stores, a two-thousand-word narrative backed by interviews. At the party, some asked if I would write a book. "I plan to," I told them. Their encouraging words resonated with me.

Sitting on the porch, watching docked boats bob in the water and palm trees sway in the light breeze, I again thought about Eldo. If he could learn to read at fifty, while balancing his health and his finances, if he could share everything he owns, giving his last dollar, then surely I could pick up a little slice of his attitude and forge a new way forward. Time to get up and get going, knowing there are helping hands all around me.

ꜱꙅ Afterword Cꙅꙅ

Volunteering in Your Community

Since I finished writing *The Mayor of Moultrie Avenue*, I have been asked for recommendations on how and where to get started as a community literacy volunteer. I know what worked for me – and for Eldo – but what might work for others of varying backgrounds and geographic locations?

For readers who are interested in becoming literacy tutors, there is no shortage of organizations (local and national) with which to volunteer. You'll need to decide whether you want to work with adult learners, as I did, or with younger learners. Consider your own interests, temperament, talents, and time available.

Are you more drawn to read with children at a local school, safe house, or homeless shelter or to volunteer with a family or adult literacy program? Are you attracted to large-scale, community-building literacy initiatives such as the One City/One County/One Book programs that have sprung up in more than four hundred locations around the country? For a list of One City One Book programs, go to en.wikipedia.org/wiki/One_City_One_Book.

Often the best place to start is your local library. The librarians there can help you locate literacy centers in your area. Local YMCAs/

YWCAs and community colleges may also offer adult literacy programs. In central Illinois, consider the Lake Land College Project PAL Adult Volunteer Literacy Program.

Finally, many faith-based organizations engage in community service; these outreach programs may include literacy. Inquire with your own community.

Selected Literacy Resources

The Barbara Bush Foundation for Family Literacy
barbarabush.org

Center for the Study of Adult Literacy
csal.gsu.edu

Frank Charles Laubach's "Each One Teach One" Literacy Program
proliteracy.org

Laubach Literacy Staff. *Teaching Adults: A Literacy Resource Book.* New York: New Reader's Press, 1994.
A collection of literacy exercises and advice for new tutors.

Literacy for All/Adult Literacy @ your library
www.ala.org/offices/literacy-all-adult-literacy-your-library
This website provides a review of data on adult literacy levels in the United States.

National Center for the Study of Adult Learning and Literacy
ncsall.net

Federal funding for the National Center for the Study of Adult Learning and Literacy (NCSALL) ended in 2007. The website, however, still makes research publications, training, and teaching resources available.

National Center on Adult Literacy
literacy.org

National Council of Teachers of English (NCTE)
ncte.org

More about Abraham Lincoln

Donald, David Herbert. *Lincoln*. New York: Touchstone, 1995.

Lincoln Log Cabin State Historic Site
lincolnlogcabin.org